Advanced Studies in Handwriting Psychology

COLLECTED WORKS OF JUNE CANOLES

EDITED BY SHEILA LOWE

Write
Choice
Ink

ESTABLISHED 2021

ISBN: 978-1-970181-54-8 (Paperback)

ASIN- (EPUB)

Write Choice Ink

www.sheilalowebooks.com

Printed in the United States of America

CONTENTS

Advanced Studies

FOREWORD

Sister June Canoles was the least nun-like person you could ever expect to meet. She was the first nun I'd ever seen wear trousers, rather than the old-fashioned traditional habit. And as someone who spent the first two years of my educational life at a convent school, I can attest that I never heard one of the sisters laugh the way June could. She lived from 1929 to 2020, and had an entrepreneurial spirit that resulted in a handwriting analysis practice and course called The Insyte Challenge. When she was 'excommunicated' from IGAS, she wore it as a badge of honor and began to use some gestalt principles in her work.

June had a great interest in company logos. Her presentation at the Asilomar Vanguard Conference in the late 1990s was educational and fun, as was her 2000 Vanguard Conference talk on The Happiness Quotient. She worked with Fortune 500 companies and for a long time, did employment analysis for Donald Trump's companies. A popular speaker, June traveled all over, dispensing their wisdom, always entertaining, with her close friend and collaborator, Sr. Harriet Dow, acting as her foil.

I became better acquainted with Sister June, as she was known, when I invited her to give a weekend seminar on the Enneagram. She was the first person I knew who used it and applied it to handwriting analysis. When she told me I was a Six I was incensed, though I understand why she thought that—I used to call her frequently to worry about something. As a dyed-in-the-wool Four, I didn't want to be like anyone else.

June wrote several monographs that many handwriting analysis students have found helpful. Long ago, she gave them over to me to sell on her behalf. Now that she is gone to that big convent in the sky (which she is no doubt running with efficiency and humor), I want to make sure her work continues, which is why I have combined several of her papers into this book, and two others in another volume in the same series.

She grew to be a dearly loved friend, and in those days before email I enjoyed her letters, which always included pertinent cartoons. She is missed by many.

Connections
The Bridge to Others

INTRODUCTION

Handwriting interpretation flows from a set of fundamental principles about the mental, physical, and emotional characteristic of the writer. When we interpret, we take each of these characteristics into consideration and attempt to determine through which of these avenues the writer views life. Obviously, all three characteristic will be apparent in the writing, but usually one or the other will predominate, giving the analyst a quick clue to the individual traits and their relationship to every other trait, making the person different from every other person.

There is no simple way to analyze handwriting as a total response; so, the expert analyst does not work in a quick, off-the-cuff way, except when someone presents a short sample and asks for a spontaneous overview. When this happens, the analyst is careful to let the person know that to guard accuracy it would be necessary to have a longer sample and more analysis time to present a total picture.

This essay deals primarily with the modes by which letters are joined—known as the connective forms. We use twenty-six letters of the alphabet to form words. Those who print for whatever reason—and there are many—deal only with the twenty-six unconnected letters, forming words with spaces between letters. actually, however, to arrive at fluency we join letters, linking them together with downstrokes and upstrokes. These are known as 'connectors' or 'connectives,' and are usually classified into four main groups: garlands, arcades, angles, and thread. a study of the combinations of these main groups in an individual's handwriting will also be of help to the analyst.

This is a starting point which includes a more precise and complicated study of the four recognizable types of connectors, some of the combinations which may be found in any one handwriting sample, a review of high and low form writing, some indication of personality traits revealed in connections, and on indication of the vocational preferences that follow from this study of traits.

CHAPTER ONE
Form, Four Main Types of Connectors

In order to think in a logical, connective fashion we link our thoughts to one another in contrast to a type of thought that is labeled 'stream-of-consciousness thinking.' Understanding the connectives and the manner in which a person uses them gives the analyst a deep look into a person's mind and his/her usual way of thinking and approaching life, as well as the needs, preferences, goals and thought patterns that distinguish this unique person from every other individual.

Knowing that much about a person gives the analyst a significant understanding of the attitudes of an individual and the likely action that will follow.

For this reason, it is important that a careful study of the connectives and their meaning be pursued in on ongoing manner by the serious analyst. When beginning any analysis, it is imperative that we give attention to the overall form level of the writer's expressive movement.

Traits may be influenced in a positive or negative way within the context of high or low form level. always consider the effect of form level in your evaluations. as well as the relationship of one trait to another.

This takes us back to a vital warning to handwriting analysts:

Always refer to the text for supportive or reductive traits. Evaluation is the key to successfully discerning the whole, dynamic personality of the writer.

High form level consists of:

▷ Good rhythm

▷ Zonal balance

▷ Originality

▷ Legibility

▷ Speed

Low form level

level lacks these qualities, resulting in a disintegrated, rigid, or contrived writing.

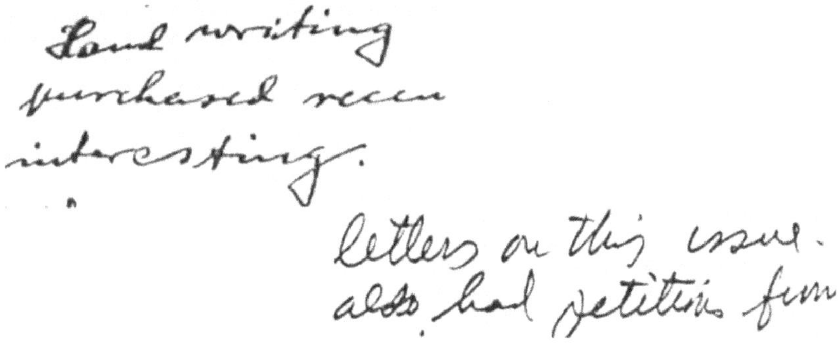

[handwritten notes]
Loud writing
purchased recent
interesting.

letters on this issue.
also had petition firm

In approaching a handwriting sample, it is advisable to give a quick look at the writing, set it aside, and ask yourself what stands out as distinctive of this sample.

Usually, your first response will be in reference to high or low form. as you look at the writing more closely you will begin to check strokes, connections, pressure, and zones in order to get the total picture. Initially, the precise analyst sees the major emphasis at first glance.

Connective forms

To begin with connections, these strokes link letters together and demonstrate the writer's social altitudes and mental processes. They also determine the flow of handwriting which, in turn, represents a connection of the writer with others, their adaptability to the world and theor degree of sociability.

In the school model, the student has been taught a connective style which is conforming. With maturity he/she is able to break away from this model and mirror his/her own value system and approach to living. When this become evident, it is possible to fit the writing into one or more of the four types of connectives being discussed.

The terms "garland," "arcade," "angle," and "thread," refer to the visual impression produced by the connective itself. Both the arcade and the garland are rounded, the one becoming the inverse of the other. The arcade is in the shape of an arch, the garland is like an open bowl:

Garlands

should be studied

Arcades

RESPONSIBILITY for the DECO

Angles

history is the fact that we sprang

Thread

*I'm convinced we first have to go
my interlive and almost certainly
period of "gay" through the crucible"
Sure enough -- we'll find out
leadership really is..*

CHAPTER TWO

The Garland

The garland is the first connective taught in the school model. We learned a high degree of connectedness between letters. Handwriting analysts need to be familiar with the Palmer Method which was the standard for many years Zaner-Bloser. A combination of the Palmer and Spencerian methods, it came on the scene somewhat later, but still influences the teaching of penmanship. Other methods, such as the D'Nealian are used throughout the United States.

A glance at the handwriting pictured in any one of these methods will show a smooth flow of connections between letters There will be no angles or threadiness. It is helpful to gain a general knowledge of the penmanship system which was part of the learning process of those whose handwriting we study. The degree of deviation from the learned system will have a great deal to say about the personality, conformity, non-conformity, originality, and independence of the writer.

A high degree of conformity to the school model is usually interpreted as the writing of a conventional person who feels comfortable in conforming to the dictates of society. A lack of conformity, on the other hand, would indicate a person with more originality.

The Garland Connection is the most used letter link in all countries that use the Latin alphabet. However, Klara

Roman reports that "until quite recently, an angular style of writing prevailed" in the teaching of handwriting in Germany.

School Models

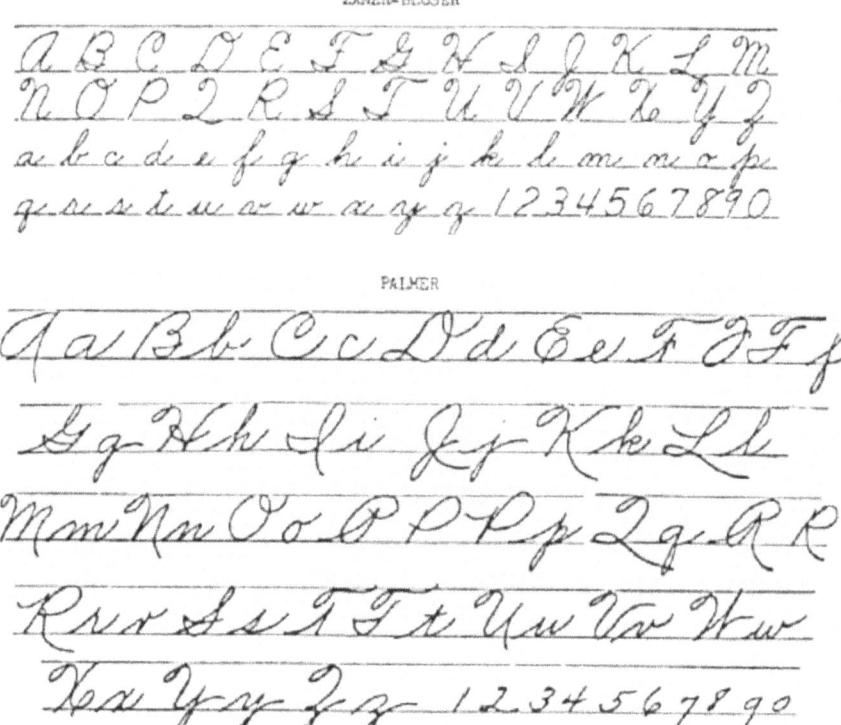

Garlands are produced when the connecting strokes are made in cup fashion, as follows:

Garland connective letters present an effortless motion which moves without friction and conflict. In the same manner, the garland writer proceeds in a kindhearted, gentle manner, avoiding struggles and conflict. This writer is less precise and more gullible than an angle writer. S/he goes with the flow, is unlikely to go against the tide, preferring to adapt rather than challenge. Generous, flexible, expressive, the garland writer needs to be needed. Although not particularly original, if the writing speed confirms it, s/he is usually a rapid thinker.

The strengths of the garland include its effortless motion which furnishes a release of tension as it moves without friction and conflict.

The weakness of the garland is that it is less precise and indicates a certain gullibility. Then what kind of a person would have writing with a high percentage of garlands? It has been quite well validated that the garland type of writer will flow with the tide, not against it, will prefer to adapt rather than to challenge. This person wants to be needed, Is generous, flexible, expressive, thinks smoothly, but is not particularly original.

In high form level or overall positive script, the writing will be distinguished by regularity and clarity. Firm strokes, pressure, and rhythm, balancing the writer's flexible nature by control and discretion.

Am I going to say

If the writing indicates low form or less positive script there will be few signs of strength, indicating that the writer is easily influenced. and responds to trivia and meaningful information In the same manner. Curiosity can become prying or meddling, while social concern will change to an interest in hearsay and idle talk.

height and breadth

There is often evidence of artificial strength (rigidity) and a need for passive control (Ed. note: do not confuse this comment with the arcade forms seen in this sample.

Garlands may also indicate a tendency toward carelessness, indifference, recklessness, and negligence.

Personality traits indicated by high and low form level writing

High Form Level	Low Form Level
Spontaneous	Superficial
Sociable	Affected
Adaptable	Gullible
Impressionable	Physically indolent
Responsive	Voluble
Receptive	Susceptible
Outer-directed	Easygoing
Frank	Deceptive

Occupational preferences - garlands

When directing garland writers in their occupational preferences the analyst concludes that these spontaneous, outer-directed, and sociable people would likely find the most satisfaction and success in one of the social, conventional, or enterprising employment opportunities such as:

Social Work, Teaching, Nursing Political activities, Reception Opportunities, Office Work, Personnel Management, Sales, Theatrical, Travel Guide, Beautician.

CHAPTER THREE

The Arcade

The opposite of garlands, arcade connective forms resemble arches, bridges, and the inverted cup. They are rounded on the top with an angle on the bottom; occasionally they are looped on the bottom.

Since this connection is made with slower movement than the garland, it suggests a writer who is more cautious and inner directed, one more closed in, like the inverted cup it resembles.

Arcade connection letters show a writer who protects against error and is efficient with words and time. The drawbacks include less spontaneity, a more calculated response, or a possible indication that appearances are more important than essence. This writer is a person who is somewhat reserved and secretive, self -oriented, and self-protective, with thought processes that are less rapid than the garland writer. He/she will usually possess a very good memory.

The strengths of the arcade include precision, control, and a need for Objectivity. The weakness of the arcades lies in the constant holding back, abruptness and tension it exhibits. Protection of his/her own interests is a priority; therefore, most of his/her responses will be carefully calculated. This writer is strongly affected by stimuli from the lower zone—the material, physical, subconscious, or instinctive needs. Therefore, s/he is less motivated by intellectual values or philosophical ideals.

In high form or positive script, the writing will show a concentration on goals and a desire to proceed with a minimum of interruptions. In fact, this writer carefully protects him/herself from interruptions. He/she possesses good manners, and depth of feeling, often relying more on intuition than on reason. The arcade writer will also have actual interest in form, aesthetics, and structures.

a great new house
house I should say.

In low form or less positive script with arcades, there will be an indication of concealment and protection shown in low and looped arcades. This may indicate dishonesty, insincerity, hypocrisy, and a tendency to plot and scheme. (Flat arcades)

Arcade writers may be shy and Inhibited, pensive, oversensitive, cautious, and impenetrable. They can also be profound and possess unusual artistic gifts. (Prominent arches)

have always thought that I
thought often confirmed by
late dictating machines.

great
evening.

Personal traits of the arcade writer indicated by high and low form level writing:

HIGH FORM	LOW FORM
Creative	Possible swindling tendencies
Diplomatic	Possible dishonest tendencies
Amiable	Possible criminal tendencies
Reserved	Hypocritical
Formal	Lacking strong values
Sympathetic	Domineering
Secretive	Manipulative
Discrete	Scheming

Occupational preferences

Since the arcade resembles an arch or a bridge and the slower form or movement suggests a writer who likely has an artistic sense of proportion and creativity, the vocational preferences to suggest would include:
Sculptors, builders, planners, architects, artists, interior designers, landscapers, photographers, dancers.

CHAPTER FOUR

The Angle

The angle is the formation that results when two lines converge and make contact at one point. It requires a deliberate, controlled, full stop at each change of direction and is, therefore, the slowest of the connections.

I worked long and hard with him

The angle benefits the writer by giving a sense of control and precision, and indicates a need for objectivity and decisiveness. Angle writers are abrupt, tense, and inclined to hold back. They are very particular about what they want, and aggressive in going after it. They rely heavily on an analytical approach to their problems. There is an indication of anxiety and some repressed emotion in the angled writing.

The angle writer is not a follower; s/he prefers to fight rather than give in. Angles are aggressive strokes and people who use them will be less conforming and less convention that arcade or garland writers.

Angle writers will expect others to meet their standards. They are less easily influenced, and more easily irritated. Tense and critical, they won't feel the need to conform to the wishes of others. They exude a powerful pent-up energy and are capable of high achievement.

In high form or positive script, angle writing indicates strong minded individuals, rugged individualists, herd workers, problem solvers, energetic and objective achievers with great mental potential. Angle writers are goal-oriented and analytical with definite points of view. They are less open and receptive than garland writers and are skeptical by nature.

There has been a long standing controversy as to whether photography is art. Painters

In less positive end/or low form script, a constant need to prove him/herself may indicate inner conflict and ego difficulties. Inflexibility, mental dogmatism or physical brutality may result If the person cannot find a positive release of these tensions. Without visible accomplishments, he/she can grow quarrelsome, blunt, cruel, and aggressive.

Personal traits or the angle writer indicated by high and low form writing:

High form	Low form
Decisive	Obstinate
Non-conforming	Abrupt
Precise	Lack of humor
Not easily influenced	Argumentative
Goal oriented	Easily irritated
Discriminating	Stubborn
Aggressive (self-starter)	Harsh
Tense	Cunning

Occupational preferences

The angle writer's aggressive, objective, decisive, argumentative, investigative traits would seem to indicate successes one of the following professionals:

Manager, Lawyer, Diplomat, Educator, Chemist, Research Analyst, Engineer, Musician, Politician, Technologist

CHAPTER FIVE

Thread/Mixed Type/Printing

THREAD: a loose, featureless, indefinite formation with only a hint of a letter form. (These forms appear both in the shaping of letters and as connectors between the letters within the word.)

The thread like form may also be the result of excessively fast writing. It could indicate a person who remains uncommitted to any one course of action.

The thread is an expressive, spontaneous stroke. It suggests minimal need for concentration and shows a person who prefers suggestion and subtlety. Thready writing within words may also warn that the writer is falling apart, or bordering on hysteria.

Thready writing persons are those who prefer spontaneity over clarity, freedom to change, avoidance of restrictions, and a path to escape difficult situations. He/she is open, broadminded, subtle, and inconsistent, disliking routine or repetition. The preference is for creative endeavors.

In high form level (positive script), the thready writer appears mentally adroit, clever, diplomatic, creative, and artistic, with the ability to change freely. The analyst will look for a fair degree of legibility, good style, firmness to offset the malleable thread, regularity, spacing, drives, motivators, integrity, pressure and realism.

In less positive or low form level script there will be indications of an individual who lacks conviction, is purposefully unclear, uncommitted, and uses his/her powers of sensitivity and penetration to take advantage. (Double agent) be on the alert for poor form, spacing, pressure. This sample was written by President Richard Nixon after he resigned from office.

HIGH FORM	LOW FORM
Spontaneous	Uncommitted
Intuitive	Inconsistent
Clever	Purposeless
Non-judgmental	Superficial
Adroit	Questioned integrity
Creative	Unstable
Great sensitivity	Indecisive
Versatility	Deceitful
	Seeks path of least resistance
	Unorganized

Occupational preferences

Since the thread writer is clever, spontaneous, and creative, vocational preferences would include: Diplomatic Positions, Politics, Sales, Artistic Endeavors

Mixed Types

It is unusual to find writing which illustrates one of the four connections totally. In most writing there are combinations of angles and garlands, arcades with angles, garlands with threads, arcades with thread, or angles with thread.

These mixed types tend to balance the traits, lending strength to the positive qualities and softening traits which might be considered negative writing which is too uniform suggests a one-sided personality. To interpret the mixes, the analyst checks closely to determine the manner and frequency of their occurrence, and finds which traits are predominant.

Garlands with arcades

This is a positive mix, as it combines the strength of the arcade with the receptivity of the garland. Many artists use this blend of connective forms.

Garlands with angles

This is another good combination with the angle strengthening the garland and the garland furnishing the relaxed and responsive traits that make it easy for the writer to present a supportive, rather than a critical opinion.

Garlands with threads

This combination presents a writer who is lacking in drive and initiative.

Arcades with angles

This mix belongs to a goal-oriented perfectionist. Although usually very successful, s/he tends to be inflexible, critical, and pompous. The arcade/angle writer is often difficult to know, intolerant, and difficult to work with.

Arcades with thread

While this mix shows a highly creative person, the combination of the secretive, self-oriented, and self-protective arcade writer with the thread writer who is often difficult to know often presents with antisocial traits. The combination could even indicate a criminal mind.

Although his place

Angles with thread

The aggressive, direct force of the angle, combined with the open-minded attitude of the thread, could provide the drive which is needed for a high degree of creativity.

PRINTING

Analysts are constantly being questioned about people who print rather than using script; so, a word about this writer is appropriate. The printer disconnects all bridges. Since the connections represent communication and emotion, the printer is distancing him/ herself from others and communicates only with figures for clarity.

The printer is usually predictable, structured, organized, objective, unemotional. His/her major emphasis is technical, not person oriented.

When analyzing printing, it is important to look for regularity and ratio which signifies the overage or above average person. Regular spacing indicates a striving for order and self -control.

Forward slant and printing presents a contradiction or conflict, showing a desire to respond to people in a spontaneous manner while disconnecting the bridge that would unite. It is possible to analyze the same patterns as in cursive writing.

Look for consistency of
- organization
- alignment of letters, words, lines and margins
- originality
- depth
- sharpness

Factors that are different
- zonal measurements
- usually no connections
- when there are connections:
    --air   --garlands
    --arcades   --angles   --thread

Suggested Reading

Amend, K. & Ruiz, H. *Handwriting Analysis, The Complete Basic Book*. Newcastle Publishing Co., Inc., North Hollywood, CA, 1980

Canoles, June, SND. *Find It More Ways, Motivations*. lnsyte, Inc, San Jose, CA, 1984

Hartford, Huntington. *You are What You Write*. Collier Books, MacMillan, New York, N.V. 1976

Hearns, Rudolph S. *Handwriting, An Analysis Through its Symbolism*. Vantage Press, Inc.• New York, N&,1979.

IGAS. *Basic Traits of Graphoanalysis*. IGAS, Inc. Chicago, IL., 1968.

IGAS. *The Encyclopedic Dictionary for Graphoanalysts* (3rd Edition}

IGAS,Inc., Chicago, IL,1984.

Karohs, Erik M. *Ambivalence as Seen In Handwriting,* V2. Pebble Beach, CA.

Mendel, Alfred 0. *Personality In Handwriting*, Stephen Daye Press, New York, NY, 1982.

Owens, Lorraine. *Different Ways To Describe Traits*. Smith-Grieves Co., Kansas City, MO, 1976.

Owens, Lorraine. *Handwriting Analysis Dictionary*, Kaleidoscope, Kansas City, MO, 1981.

Roman, Klara G. *Handwriting, a Key To Personality*, Pantheon books, New York, NY, 1952.

The Coping
Mechanisms

Coping Mechanisms

Fear, Anxiety and Trauma

Assessment of the strength and number of fears and defenses in a handwriting is the core of any handwriting analysis because it determines the security and the maturity level of the writer. It is not the fears, anxiety, and the traumas a person suffered that determines how the individual will behave in the long run, but how the person copes.

An individual has three ways of coping with setbacks in life. 1) s/he can defend the Self in wholesome ways, adjusting to protect the ego; 2) s/he can defend the Self by resisting (fighting back) and using an attack method, or 3) by escaping (flight from reality) using a denial method.

Fear, anxiety, and trauma begin in early childhood. They may be the result of a broken home, a death in the family or severe treatment from a parent or sibling in the family. Some fears are necessary for self-preservation such as the fear of fire, the fear of water, the fear of falling, or the fear of hunger. This presentation is about emotional scars that result in insecurities.

When these fears, anxieties and traumas appear in one's handwriting we can be certain that they impact the person's whole life in some degree. The strength of the scores for any of these specific identifiers will indicate to the analyst that the person is still suffering from his/ her early painful imprint.

The exciting part of the handwriting analyst's work is in discovering that, in time, and certainly with counseling and/or love some of these fears, anxieties and traumas can be completely washed from a person's script, and if not completely, at least the scores will be lessened to a significant degree. The analyst is then left with an opportunity to encourage and congratulate the writer on her I his journey toward wholeness.

In some respects, you will find that this chapter is a review for you because we will be pulling together the Specific identifiers that represent the fears and defenses in the handwriting. You will immediately realize that you have learned most of them in previous chapters. Now, however, these specific identifiers will be put into their rightful place as part of the coping mechanisms. You will now be able to evaluate them in relation to the whole personality and determine if the writer is secure and mature. Further, you will know if the writer is still dealing with the past and you will be able to bring comfort to the present.

This is information is not intended to be a psychological study, we will present in a straightforward, uncomplicated manner. The information is to be used to understand the writer. When working one-on-one with a person this information can be imparted to build understanding. Do *not* include it in personnel reports unless it affects the job description. In that case, unless you have a medical or psychology license, do not diagnose, only describe the behavior.

Note: It is important that the analyst who is not a counselor or a psychologist recommend to anyone whose handwriting exhibits severe problems in the fears and defenses areas be referred to a professional who can adequately handle that type of deep-seated problem. Working in an area where we are not trained may not only leave the analyst vulnerable to a lawsuit, but could unknowingly cause damage to the person, who may be more emotionally disturbed than the analyst realizes.

We itemize eleven specific identifiers representing early fears and anxieties.

Basically, we can assume that emotional disturbances in children are rooted in fears based on insecurities. Everyone has to work through a certain amount of insecurity in her or his life. Generally, everyone has at least two, three, or four fear areas to overcome in a lifetime. Sometimes the analyst will only see the residue of these early fears.

Use a scoring chart from one to seven, (seven being the highest), it would be quite normal to have several fears appear in a script, but scoring on the low side of the chart. (These will be found in the two or three columns of the chart). It is still normal for persons to have one of their fears score high, (in a four or five column) on your chart. The lower the scores are on your 'fear chart,' the more you can assume that the person you are analyzing has worked through their early childhood insecurities.

Remember: A certification in handwriting analysis and the knowledge that you are able to obtain from a script does not meet the qualification of a counselor or psychologist unless you have obtained a degree in these areas.

The defense traits as wholesome protectors, resistance (fight) and escape (flight), will be presented after the fear and trauma sections of this chapter.

1. **Desire for attention** is an unfulfilled need for recognition, approval and/ or to be appreciated by others. This can be either real or imagined by the child. When the at-

tention given a child falls short of the child's need, it is natural for the child to try to gain more emotional security. You have already learned that the stroke for this specific indicator is a final upswing at the end of words. When this compensation for unmet needs becomes very strong the finals will grow increasingly larger indicating that the child, now an adult, will play excessively for attention in one way or another.

2. **Self-criticism and blame** may start early in life or come later in life, but it always indicates some type of guilt feelings. The person looks back on some painful event with disapproval. The final stroke in a word also moves back ward but in a stabbing, punishing fashion, often in the crossing of the "t" from right to left. The person may vocalize this displeasure internally or become involved in high risk activities. Basically, this blame is unfounded because it is so often just the result of the human condition. Of course, the weight of the stroke, in this Specific identifier and/or the length of its back-to-self stabbing will indicate its punishing effect.

3. **Indecisiveness** is the fear of finality and causes the person to vacillate between alternatives. It is indicated by weak, feathering endings and determines the arrangement, form, and movement of the writing. This fear trait can be construed to be a form of self-presentation because the person's view of making a decision as an entrapment which offers no escape.

4. **Self-consciousness** more often than not comes from having been put down and ridiculed as a child either in the home or at school. A child must be corrected and guided through life, but if the child is humiliated or made the brunt of jokes because of some "difference," then the child is likely to suffer for many years. This specific indicator

can be recognized by the last hump of an "m" or "n" extending higher than the preceding humps. The higher the last hump and the frequency with which it is seen in a writing determines its strength.

5. **Self-underestimation** is the lack of self-esteem which is an essential element for successful living and the ability to reach one's potential. When a child does not receive enough early emotional security s/he will struggle with the fear of failure for years. This Specific indicator can be seen quickly in low "t" bar crossing. In more extreme cases the crossings are below the mid zone letters. Often the analyst will see outstanding talent in a handwriting only to realize that, in the eyes of the individual, this talent is very underestimated. This, of course, stifles the development of many a gifted person.

6. **Sensitiveness to criticism** is the fear of disapproval resulting from repeated hurt or criticism from an early age. A child's greatest need is to be loved and valued. Many children, if not most, hear more criticism from their parents and teachers than praise. The specific indicator is a large loop on either the 11d" or the "t" formation. The larger these two loops are, coupled with a lively imagination (lower zone loops), the greater the impact of this fear trait. Every individual is sensitive to disapproval, but most are able to evaluate the criticism in perspective. The overly sensitive individual will "see" or experience criticism where there may be none, resulting in a feeling of inadequacy.

7. **Rejection** shows that the child fears the loss of affection and/ or status. This is seen in the personal pronoun I." It can indicate poor bonding with one or other of the parents or both. Without the feeling of being accepted, receiving affection or the building of self-worth, there is no bonding and then the child, and later the adult, is like a ship with-

out a rudder. The writer stumbles through life and in and out of one relationship after another. Unfortunately, this Specific identifier is a direct result of the child's perception of the parents. It may not be a true perception of the parenting that actually took place.

8. **Repression** chokes self-expression, buries feelings and cuts off spontaneity. Retraced "m's" and "n's" are the main indicators of this complicated fear. It is complicated because it is so submerged in the unconscious that it is unrecognizable. Even though suppression and repression are in some ways similar they are different. Suppression, as a process, is a conscious and intermittent, holding back of emotional expressions (a squeezed writing form) while repression is an unconscious and constant type of "wiping out" (going over a downstroke with an upstroke) of hurtful memories.

9. **Fear of rivalry** is basically a fear of not being lovable. It consists of comparing oneself with others and coming up short. This can be the result of parent and/ or teacher input or just that the child has taken it upon herself/himself to react in this way.

10 **Withdrawal**, seen in reclined slant, results when a child's spontaneity is stifled or the child experiences some form of rejection and s/he emotionally withdraws. This is a form of protection, writing in a backward slant, signifies repressed emotions so that the child now views life in relation to herself / him self.

11 **Worry** is feeling of distress and/ or anxiety in regard to the present or the future. Seen in extra loops in "the legs" of the "M's" and "N's." It is a sad fact that worry does not change a thing in a person's life.

Trauma may or may not be part of childhood experiences. A trauma occurs after a shattering experience such as a loss of a sibling, loved one or a divorce, to mention a few. Some kind of trauma has occurred when there are split (stenciled looking) letters, twists in letters and/or a general trauma in the handwriting.

Of course, these latter can also indicate a physical, medical and/ or drug related problem, so it is well to speak directly with the person in order to determine with which of these situations you are dealing. The "d" is directly related to **self-feel** and if this is twisted or bent in any fashion, it is a sure sign that the child has experienced some abuse either psychologically or physically. Other signs are soldering, stabs in ovals, and/or under strokes, phallic signs, clothesline garlands, inner bubbles, dark spots, some letters rubbing up against each other and claws.

Defenses

The ego must be protected at all costs. All children and adults seek approval, recognition, and acceptance from their peers. Much emotional energy is exerted defensively to maintain these needs. According to the measure of maturity and security the individual has attained, choices are made about the manner to defend oneself. The major wholesome defenses (adjusters) that we can determine in handwriting analysis are eighteen in number. When these adjusters fail to sustain the ego, the individual will automatically make a choice of either resisting (fight) or escaping (flight) in order to survive.

It is desirable to have high scores in the wholesome ego defenses and low scores in the resistant/escape defenses. Of course, any scores which are abnormally high would be a "red flag" for the analyst and possibly a "stopper" when it comes to realizing an individual's potential, e.g., too much caution would stop a person "dead in their tracks" or too much "humor" might be a facade covering inner conflicts and / or too much philosophical development-a "cop out"-so the analyst must always be vigilant, assessing the whole to determine how secure and mature the individual is.

REMEMBER: One specific identifier which should not be high is perfectionism. As it moves toward a five score there can be genuine problems with the flexibility so necessary for one to move with the flow of life.

Graphs on the following pages:

Graphs #1 and #2 scores are in a normal range for fear traits.

Graphs #3 and #4 have several low scored fears and one rather high scored fear trait. These are still within the normal range of fear traits.

Graphs #5 and #6 have very high scored fear traits and would be of concern to the analyst. Immediately the analyst should move to the defense columns to see if the personality can sustain and properly cope with such a great amount of fear.

DEFENSES: WHOLESOME EGO PROTECTORS
(Many high scores are desirable)

1 2 3 4 5 6 7		1 2 3 4 5 6 7	
	Caution		Caution
	Decisiveness	2	Decisiveness
	Dignity		Dignity
	Diplomacy		Diplomacy
	Fluidity		Fluidity
	Humor		Humor
	Independent thinking		Independent thinking
	Intuitiveness		Intuitiveness
	* Narrow-mindedness		* Narrow-mindedness
	Objectivity (vertical slant)		Objectivity (vertical slant)
	* Perfectionism		* Perfectionism
	Persistence		Persistence
	Philosophical Imagination		Philosophical Imagination
	Positiveness		Positiveness
	Pride		Pride
	* Selectivity		* Selectivity
	Self-control		Self-control
	Yieldingness		Yieldingness

* Become negative defenses if scores are high

We Identify Eighteen Wholesome Ego Defenses (adjusters and protectors)

1. **Caution** is made with a long straight stroke at the end of a word or signature. It protects the individual from making mistakes. It signifies one last look before taking action so as to minimize the chance of an imprudent risk. The stronger the pressure and the length of the stroke indicate its strength.

2. **Decisiveness** is recognized by a firm, blunt ending stroke in word. (It should also be evaluated along with organization, consistency, simplification, speed, legibility, and space and MZ regularity. By making a quick and firm choice, the individual presents a confident attitude which protects them him from censure.

3. **Dignity** is indicated by medium height retraced "d" and "t" stems, the individual finds security in acting in a proper, established manner. This assures him / her that there will be little to no criticism from others.

4. **Diplomacy** is observed by a slowly diminishing MZ at the end of words, sentences, or signatures. It loses its strength if the letters shrink too dramatically. The individual who uses this specific indicator is able to influence situations without seeming to do so and thus protect and save the ego from harm.

5. **Fluidity** is a flowing movement that moves gracefully from one zone to another, joining strokes in an original way. As a specific indicator, it facilitates smooth mental or emotional adjustment without causing friction.

6. **Humor** is shown by an initial "wavy" stroke generally beginning on capital "H", "M" and "N." It is a sign that the writer can laugh at her/himself, or laugh even when the joke is on her I himself, seeing both sides of a situation

and/ or defusing what otherwise might be an unpleasant situation.

7. **Independent thinking** is evident by observing how short the "t" bars and "d" stems are made. An independent thinker is by definition a non-conformist. By setting standards other than what is generally accepted the person is not disconcerted by what others think.

8. **Intuitiveness** is seen in the syllabic breaks between letters in word formations. It is a natural adjuster since the individual instinctively senses how to say the right thing at the right time. This protects the ego against embarrassing mistakes.

9. **Narrow-mindedness** is basically the closing of the "e" formation so that it looks like an "i" and is supported by closed "a's" and "o's." When an individual closes her / his mind to new information, it excludes emotionally painful thoughts and ideas. The ego is not threatened if the person refuses to entertain any threatening new information.

10. **Objectivity** is generally attributed to the vertical slant writer and in the inclined slant when any letter is consistently vertical. The vertical slant writer controls expressiveness and strikes a balance between possible alternatives thus protecting the ego from costly mistakes.

11 **Perfectionism** is seen in perfectly formed letters on an exact baseline. It operates as a protector and an adjuster in that it protects the individual from making mistakes and helps to stave off disapproval, but it also stifles spontaneity, so a low score, not a high one, is suggested.

12. **Persistence** is shown by the "tie" formation in any letter. These can be found in many MZ letters, such as the "f" or "t's" and/or in a capital letter such as a "H." The number of "tie" formations will give strength to this specific

identifier as an adjuster and protector. When an individual refuses to give up in the face of difficulties she/ he refuses to succumb to fear.

13. **Philosophical Imagination** is seen in well-developed UZ loops. Having a well-balanced personality as indicated in the development of all of the three zones in writing helps the individual to view life squarely and adjust adequately. A philosophical outlook helps to assess the past, present and the future as a whole, insulating the ego from taking painful situations too seriously

14. **Positiveness** looks much like the specific identifier, economy, since it is a final stroke that comes down to the baseline at the end of a word. However, the specific identi-fier, positiveness, is a final stroke that not only comes down to the baseline but does so with a very strong, defi-nite ending.

This type of individual speaks in an emphatic tone of voice. This specific identifier is not to be confused with stubborn-ness which goes farther than positiveness since there is no possibility of change (a resistant defense). Speaking with conviction and taking a firm stand on an opinion, does not mean that the individual cannot change once more infor-mation comes to light. Positiveness is a protector in that others believe that the person knows what she/ he is talk-ing about because of the definiteness of tone. Others tend to back away and seldom even question those who make positive statements.

15. **Pride** is shown in relatively tall "d" and "t" stems is the desire to do what is expected to one's best ability. Pride sets a standard for the individual and the individual feels that what is done speaks to whom s/he as a person. Doing

things right protects the ego since pride expects others to think well of her/his conduct.

16. **Selectivity** is identified by narrow LZ loops. This specific identifier, based on fear, acts as a protector. By picking and choosing friends carefully and with similar interests there are no surprises.

17. **Self-control** can be determined by evaluating an arched "t" bar crossing. This "hat-like" bowed stroke signals that the writer is adding extra strength to her/ his will power for protection in some area or other.

18. **Yieldingness** is often found in a final rounded "s" formation, "r", "h" and "b" formations, a "soft p," flattened "m's" and "n's" or any formation that lacks definition. It acts as a protector against friction by giving in to those more powerful than the self. This, of course, has to be evaluated to determine whether the yieldingness is used as a defense or is the result of weakness.

RESISTANCE: (Fight) DEFENSES

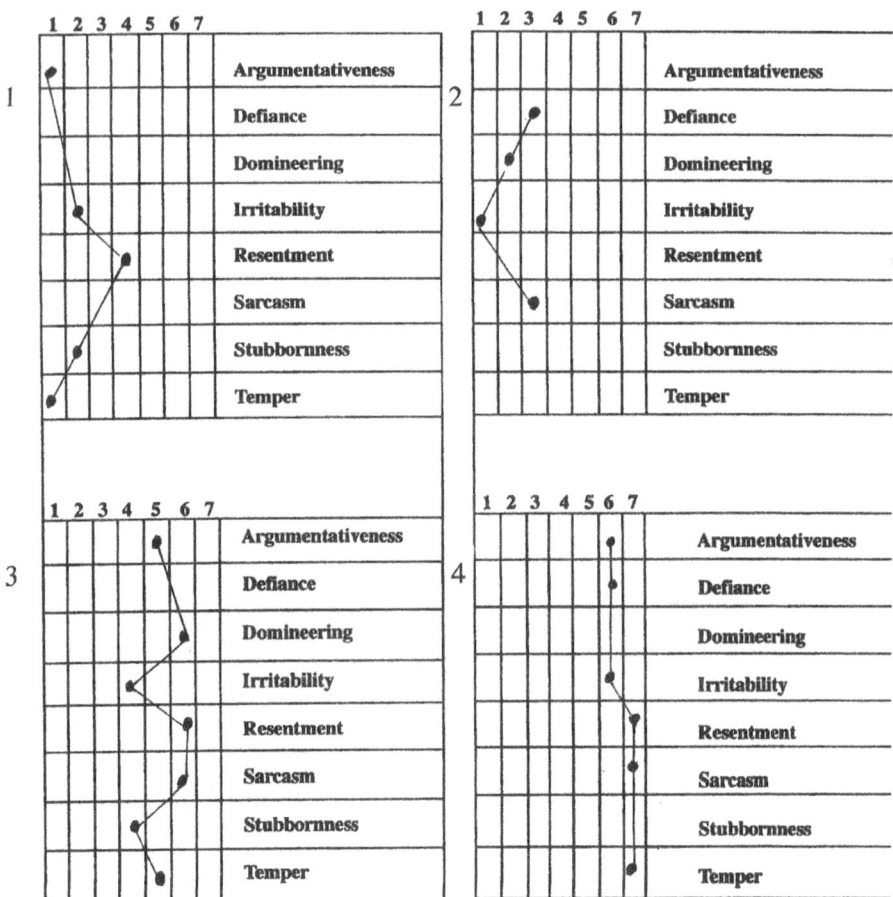

Graphs #1 and #2 scores are in a normal range for resistance.

Graphs #3 and #4 scores indicate frustration and, therefore, unhappiness in some area of the writer's life.

There are Eight Resistance (fight) Defenses that we can identify.

These eight significant identifiers indicate frustration. High scores would indicate intense frustration. The Wholesome Ego Protectors are usually sufficient for a person to maintain emotional balance and to feel secure. If a person finds her/himself in a very unproductive, unsatisfactory, and unhappy situation where there is little recourse or hope and feels backed into a comer, then either the resistance or the escape defenses will take over. Each person has a preference to choose to fight or flee in these situations.

High scores are red flags for the analyst. In a well-balanced writing the fight and flight defenses are few and the scores are low. We all need these back up defenses of fight and flight, but they should be in the background of our personality (two or three of them is normal) but the scores for them should be on the low side of the scale. It is also quite normal for a person to have at least one fairly strong score in both the fight area and the flight area.

At the beginning of this chapter we said that this is the core to any handwriting analysis. This is so not because of the fears presented above nor even the whole some ego defenses also presented above, but because one quick glance at the areas of fight and flight will tell you immediately how secure and mature the person is, how settled, how balanced, and how happy the person is in her / his present situation at home and/ or at work High scores indicate trouble. Low resistance scores are not only desirable but will give you a quick "Happiness Quotient."

It is also true that if the person you are analyzing has not developed many high scored Wholesome Ego Protections there is going to be too strong a reliance on the Resistance and Escape traits and, of course, this will mean that the person does not function well in society and/ or is unable to be peaceful and productive in the work place. So, you see how important it is for you to memorize the Eight Significant Resistance Identifiers and the Thirteen Significant Escape Identifiers.

One of the most important questions an analyst must constantly ask her/ himself is why? Why is this person angry? Why is this person hiding from reality? Why is this person not productive? Why is this person insecure? Why is this person off balance? Why is this person so unhappy and frustrated?

We cannot, as analysts, diagnose problems. However, it helps our analysis to be able to understand where the person has been, what has he/ she overcome and what is causing pain and failure. Certainly, in personnel work we can say very little, but when we work with people one-on-one it is very helpful to be able to compassionately let the person know our findings, along with their strengths and possibilities.

> **Reminder**: All of the specific identifiers in the eight resistance (fight) areas indicate that the writer attacks to defend the self.

1. **Argumentativeness** is generally found in the small "p" formation. It is identified as a point made higher than the buckle of the "p." This point may be made by a straight downward stroke from the UZ or a beginning upward approach stroke. The argumentativeness is intensified if the "p" has a stiff up stroke to it which adds resentment or a deep breakaway stroke which gives it aggressiveness. When we observe a loop on top of the buckle, the writer is a fluid arguer and is gathering more information to present as you are trying to make your point.

Sometimes we see the buckle pulled back into the "p" formation itself as if to hide. This means that the writer is trying to stifle her/ his need to defend the self by arguing. The argumentative writer basically feels that to be wrong is to lose face. There are certainly times when a friendly argument clarifies and defines ideas. What we have in the Significant Identifier of argumentativeness is a resistance trait to justify the writer's position regardless of right or wrong. Constant arguing signals a basic insecurity which, when used as an active resistance, suggests hostility in a greater or lesser degree. depending on other aspects in the writing.

2. **Defiance** can be seen in a writing that has a high "k" buckle that rises above the MZ area. This specific identifier can also be seen in a capital made in the middle or at the end of a word. When the buckle of the "k" rises completely out of the MZ area (action area) and is in the UZ area it may simply represent thoughts of defiance rather than defiance itself. Defiance is a rebellion against authority figures of real or perceived earlier injustices.

The writer may have this Specific identifier but never show it unless the "nerve" that sparked the defiance at an earlier time is pressed upon again. Then the defiant reaction, that others take to be a burst of anger, shows itself for what it is by bringing up all kinds of past injustices unrelated to the present situation. Only by evaluating the whole writing will the analyst know if this is just an "on guard attitude" or an easily activated rebellion in the personality.

3. **Domineering** is indicated by a downward slanted, spur-like "t" bar. The domineering individual is usually called "bossy or demanding" by others. It is a sign that these writers are very frustrated with their own self and/or life. Because these writers cannot get their own personal life in order they try to get other people's lives in order to make

themselves feel better. This is a specific identifier which is a futile means of controlling others and is generally quite overt and easy to ascertain.

4. **Irritability** can be seen by "i" and "j" dots that are made with stabbing motions. When the jabbing motion is pointed to the left it is likely that the writer is unhappy with her/himself. When the jabbing motions are pointed toward the right, it is more likely that this is directed at others. This is a milder resentment-specific identifier than the others, but it can be quite unpleasant. It may mean that the writer is over involved, pushing her / himself too hard or is in an unpleasant situation at home or at work.

5. **Resentment** when very strong, can easily be picked up by the analyst by running the eyes down the left margin. This specific identifier shows stiff up strokes at the beginning of many or all words in the text. When these stiff up strokes come from below the line of writing they are indicative of deep surging resentment and the writer is likely to be "touchy."

All of these stiff upstrokes indicate that the writer's guards are up against being unjustly imposed upon. This imposition may be real or imagined in the writer's mind. Certainly, this trait began with someone taking advantage of the writer somewhere along the line, but now, when the stroke is consistent in the writing, the writer views all persons as perched to take advantage of her I him at any moment.

6. **Sarcasm** can be seen by the sharp point at the end of a "t" bar crossing. Generally, the writer who makes this specific indicator unconsciously wants to punish the recipient of the barbed remark out of her I his own feelings of inadequacy.

The "sting" is an offensive form of protection and a way of belittling the other person in order to bring her / him down to the writer's level. However, it is well to realize that sarcasm can be used both defensively or offensively. When there are no other high scored resistant traits the analyst can assume that the sarcasm seen in the writing is merely there to protect and is not necessarily activated often.

7. **Stubbornness** is a "tent" formation primarily under the letters "t" and "d" and in some "m's" and "n's." This specific identifier must have a "braced look" to qualify as stubbornness. When stubbornness is used as a resistance trait, it indicates a refusal to yield, even in the face of reason. It is a face saving measure to protect the ego by refusing to admit that there may be a mistake in judgment.

8. **Temper** can primarily be seen when a "t" bar is made to the right of the "t" stem. The stroke is not grounded but free flowing because it has missed its mark. Some of these temper strokes are in the form of a "tick" in that they are a quick angle attached to a capital letter. These specific indicators rep resenting temper and frustration are signs of a tendency toward underlying temper by an angry person habitually on the alert.

A word about anger in particular and controllers in general: Anger can reside in strange places and its sister, "control", has many faces. A person can control by sickness, by needing special foods, by tears, by being late, by putting things off, by incessant talking or laughing. These are not always easy for an analyst to pick up quickly in the writing, but these often become evident in a one-on-one hand writing evaluation session. Every analyst should read about anger and its many faces. Once one of the "faces" is seen, try to find its mark in the script.

Acura provides sampling services tailored to the specific needs of our clients.

2

to make a long story short raised ten. children. my kids, her kids and or Kids till my Kid, your kids and or Kid to be quiet.

3

Perhaps they feel uncomfortable having woman on their team, but I am content leading them and not being accepted as one of their peers.

4   I am writing in regard to

5   'he ' leadeth ' me ' besides ' the

6   I love to travel

7   that the writing is a little

8   this coming Wednesday.

ESCAPE: (Flight) DEFENSES

ESCAPE: (flight) DEFENSES

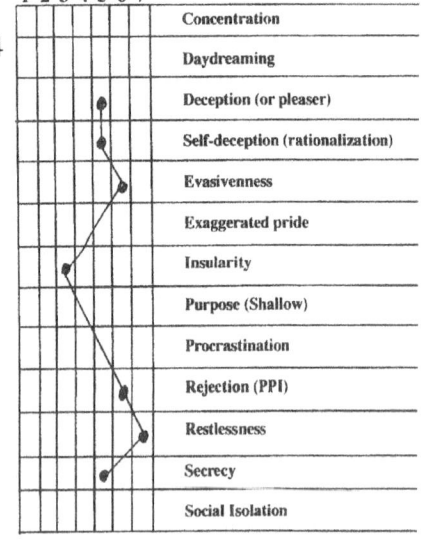

There are Twelve Escapes (flight) that we can identify.

As we have said above, the ego must be protected at all costs. If the wholesome ego adjusters break down and the individual is not inclined to fight for her/ his rights then it becomes imperative that the individual escape from the pain of reality by using denial. As Scott Peck mentions in his book, *The Road Less Traveled*, it is more painful in the long run to avoid difficulties than it is to face them right away.

In our discussion of fears, anxiety, and trauma we pointed out that these defensive forces affect our lives in various ways. We tend to build up our defenses one after another without even realizing that we are doing so. Here the analyst's ability to help another see these defensive drives which change a personality and realize that he/ she does not need to go to such great lengths to solve problems will help to stabilize a fearful personality.

Many adults do not realize that their self-esteem is at a low ebb because they have formed a low opinion of themselves, their abilities, their gifts. Not daring to aspire to their optimum gifts puts them in the unenviable position of turning to the opinions of others to learn about themselves.

Creating an idealized image of themselves only leads to more injury. They spend their time being hostile to those who seem to have gifts they lack, avoiding anyone who, in their opinion, is superior to them in some way. This leads them to ignore their creative abilities, and innate attractiveness as they step back and take refuge in isolation and pretended dignity.

Fear usually proceeds from conflicts people have not been able to resolve. The compassionate analyst can guide them to personality integration through suggesting that they solve their problems in a more secure and mature fashion.

1. **Concentration** is easily ascertained by looking and measuring the MZ; concentration is necessary for each of us in a greater or lesser degree, but when concentration is used as an escape, it is focused on the self to the exclusion of all else. This can cause emotional problems. If the MZ measurement is less than 1/16 it is important to evaluate how healthy the person is in regard to the wholesome ego protectors indicated. Adjusters showing high scores and resistance and escapes having low scores depicts a secure person.

2. **Daydreaming** when the "t" bar floats above the "t" stem the writer's goals are unconnected to reality. What better way to escape from painful reality of what might have been, than to dream of all that might someday be by building castles in the air?

3. **Deception** is indicated by two inner loops on an "a," "o," or a "d." When these inner loops are large there is more chance that the person just wants to be accepted and will say whatever it takes to make this happen. While this certainly is a form of lying, it is not as serious as when the inner two loops are very small and tightly made into a "bow tie" effect. This type of deceit is more insidious because it is more intentional.

Deceit is a result of fear, the fear of being exposed as not smart enough, good enough or worthy of another's love and respect. As an escape it points to insecurity, even if it is a bad habit left over from childhood, it is self-defeating and lowers all other character scores. When working one-on-one with a client it is possible for the analyst to point out, compassionately, how unnecessary this trait is in relation to the total personality and the writer's potential.

4. **Self-deception** — rationalization is identified as having an inner left loop within a circle letter, "a," "o," "d," or "g." The deception is not projected outward toward another but inward toward the self. It is the self that is deceived. The writer unconsciously covers over some of the facts of a situation by denying that she/ he had any part in it at all.

It is important to note that the person does not intend to deceive others but only to deceive the self. It is just too painful for the individual to admit some blame in a given situation. Most people recognize when a person is using this escape mechanism. It takes a great deal of security to own up to one's part in a failed situation.

5. **Evasiveness** made with an inner loop that moves along with and "hugs" the initial loop of the "a" formation. It is a protective procedure that comes from insecurity and a method of side stepping reality because of real or perceived pain.

6. **Exaggerated** pride appears generally in "t's" and "d's" that are excessively tall for the script. It can also be indicated in any of the UZ letters that appear excessively elongated. Exaggerated pride signifies an extreme need for approval coming from feelings of inferiority. Since the writer does not experience approval from others, s/he compensates for this real or imagined disapproval by exaggerated self-approval.

Some who have this specific identifier have had lonely childhoods where they have had to go into their heads for mental approval. The result is that now he or she puts on an air of superiority which makes it hard for others to relate to him or her. Often these writers will sell themselves higher than they are able to produce

7. **Insularity** seen by the analyst as very small, tight loop formations at the end of the LZ. Since the return of the LZ

loop indicates fulfilling relationships, these truncated LZ loops signify unsuccessful personal and social relationships. The writer who has tried and failed in relationships over and over again, will begin to withdraw into the self to protect the ego resulting in an unhealthy situation. Professional help should be recommended, depending on the amount and the intensity of these small LZ loops.

8. **Purpose** (shallow) is represented by a "dish-like" cross bar on a "t" formation. This "caved in crossing" indicates one form of directional pressure. The "dish-like" crossing must be seen on a free standing "t" to qualify, not on a fluid "t" moving into an "h" formation.

Because the cross bar is "caved in" the pressure is coming from above and indicates a writer as having experienced someone more powerful than her / himself pressuring the person into submission. Now, if writer is in another like situation she/ he may quickly leave, deserting a job or a relationship. Some analysts define this as "shallow," which has some merit, but actually it can be seen as a "wound" that acts as an emotional escape when undue pressure is experienced again in the person's life. This does translate as a risk factor in a personal or personnel situation.

9. **Procrastination** can be found when a "t" bar does not reach the place of crossing the stem. A writer who makes this type of delayed "t" crossing is procrastinating because of fear; the fear of not doing the work satisfactorily, the fear of being criticized after the work is completed, or some other fear of being ridiculed which is generally unfounded.

10. **Restlessness** can be quickly seen by examining the LZ of a writing sample. This restless stroke is a prolonged downward thrust of a "y" or "g." This significant identifier is essentially one of constantly being on the move, (after all

one can't hit a moving target), unconsciously desiring to run away from a painful situation.

11. **Secrecy** is shown by a final tied loop made on the right side of an "a" or an "o" formation. Secretiveness is a conscious desire to withhold information for one reason or another. The writer does not try to deceive or mislead but just withholds information. This is because she/ he realizes that there are problems, but does not feel it is necessary to share them. Generally, the problems are of a personal nature and happily, as the writer works these problems, the secretive loop disappears from the writing. The strength of this Significant Identifier de pends on the frequency of the stroke and the size of the loop.

12. **Social isolation** spacing is determined by large word or line spacing in the writing. When the word spacing is larger than average, the writer finds too much contact distressing and has difficulty communicating. When the line spacing is larger than average, the need for privacy is even more pronounced. Social isolation, being a fear of close contact, is a protection against the pain that social contacts inevitably cause every individual from time to time.

REMEMBER: All twelve specific identifiers in this area mean that the writer will avoid reality to defend the self.

1   You made the archives in tonight's Register. Psquirrini! what sort of an achievement that is in recent decisions. Life in Watsonville remains the same — more or less. The present city council thinks about paving our agricultural land for housing.

2   harmony - that where there is error, I may bring truth - that where there is

3   sending the halter — thank you so much for — bad rope. I'm so delighted to hear Bridgette is happy, healthy, and trimming down

4   forms together philosophically justify the integrity of the

5

2o anguish, superlative; angry adj; angrier comp.
3o empty adj; emptier comp; emptiest superlative

6

response to my request for information.
would "like" to try your "drop-in hour," as it

7

maybe? In reviewing the evaluation
and pondering the past, one thing did
pop out: Until age two my family

8

Old paint on canvas, as it ages,
sometimes becomes transparent. When that
happens it is possible, in some pictures, to see
the original lines: a tree will show through a woman

When we find persons who come to us *trapped in feelings of fear and inadequacy*, we have the ability to calm them, and help them recognize the "why" of the early painful situations in their lives. We can then point out the many *adjustment defenses* that they have which protect them from harm. We can assure them that they have survived very well in the past, and suggest what to use for help in their future.

Working with persons *trapped in feelings of frustration,* we will be able to ask them just how happy they are in their present situations. We can then help them to realize that attacking, to defend themselves, creates more problems than it solves.

9

I like to make more

10

Thank you very much for taking the time to look at my handwriting and tell me what it says.

11

I really enjoy the work, enjoy working with people. Learning new things, keeping busy. I feel I have a good attitude about dental health,

12

I am working on the meditation and am curious to see what it will bring. Although it doesn't seem probable that I'll be able to take the classes

When we see persons *who are running from reality*, we are able to explain the fact that they are just postponing the inevitable and prolonging the pain. Scott Peck points out in his book *The Road Less Traveled,* that one of the great truths is that life is difficult! Once we come to this realization, we have the ability to transcend it. "Life is a series of problems;" "Do we want to moan about them or solve them?"

We all try to avoid rather than face pain. Unfortunately, if we use substitutes such as attacking and escaping "the substitute itself ultimately becomes more painful than the legitimate suffering it was designed to avoid."

> *Remember: Attacking and escaping, when in the high score range, are areas where the balance and the emotional health of the person can be measured. Excessive use of either attack or escape, alerts the analyst to the fact the person needs professional help. It is well, for the analyst, to have the business cards of reputable counselors and psychologists ready to hand out.*

In closing, let us not forget that fear is not a reality—only love is a reality. Ruth Holmes once pointed out in one of her presentations that the letters that make up the word FEAR stand for False Evidence Appearing Real.

> ***Monk****: I understand that when a lion seizes upon his opponent, whether it is a hare or an elephant, he makes an exhaustive use of his power; pray tell me what is this power?*
>
> ***Master****: The spirit of sincerity (literally, the power of 'not deceiving').*

Sincerity—that is, not-deceiving—means "putting forth one's whole being," technically known as "the whole being in action" ... in which nothing is kept in reserve, nothing is expressed under disguise, nothing goes to waste. When a person lives like this, he is said to be a golden-haired lion; he is the symbol of virility, sincerity, wholeheartedness; he is divinely human.

DT. Suziki, Zen Buddhism and Its Influence on Japanese Culture, The Eastern Buddhist Society (Kyoto), 1938.

The Coping Mechanisms

Coping Mechanisms

Fear, Anxiety and Trauma

Assessment of the strength and number of fears and defenses in a handwriting is the core of any handwriting analysis because it determines the security and the maturity level of the writer. It is not the fears, anxiety, and the traumas a person suffered that determines how the individual will behave in the long run, but how the person copes.

An individual has three ways of coping with setbacks in life. 1) s/he can defend the Self in wholesome ways, adjusting to protect the ego; 2) s/he can defend the Self by resisting (fighting back) and using an attack method, or 3) by escaping (flight from reality) using a denial method.

Fear, anxiety, and trauma begin in early childhood. They may be the result of a broken home, a death in the family or severe treatment from a parent or sibling in the family. Some fears are necessary for self-preservation such as the fear of fire, the fear of water, the fear of falling, or the fear of hunger. This presentation is about emotional scars that result in insecurities.

When these fears, anxieties and traumas appear in one's handwriting we can be certain that they impact the person's whole life in some degree. The strength of the scores for any of these specific identifiers will indicate to the analyst that the person is still suffering from his/ her early painful imprint.

The exciting part of the handwriting analyst's work is in discovering that, in time, and certainly with counseling and/or love some of these fears, anxieties and traumas can be completely washed from a person's script, and if not completely, at least the scores will be lessened to a significant degree. The analyst is then left with an opportunity to encourage and congratulate the writer on her I his journey toward wholeness.

In some respects, you will find that this chapter is a review for you because we will be pulling together the Specific identifiers that represent the fears and defenses in the handwriting. You will immediately realize that you have learned most of them in previous chapters. Now, however, these specific identifiers will be put into their rightful place as part of the coping mechanisms. You will now be able to evaluate them in relation to the whole personality and determine if the writer is secure and mature. Further, you will know if the writer is still dealing with the past and you will be able to bring comfort to the present.

This is information is not intended to be a psychological study, we will present in a straightforward, uncomplicated manner. The information is to be used to understand the writer. When working one-on-one with a person this information can be imparted to build understanding. Do *not* include it in personnel reports unless it affects the job description. In that case, unless you have a medical or psychology license, do not diagnose, only describe the behavior.

Note: It is important that the analyst who is not a counselor or a psychologist recommend to anyone whose handwriting exhibits severe problems in the fears and defenses areas be referred to a professional who can adequately handle that type of deep-seated problem. Working in an area where we are not trained may not only leave the analyst vulnerable to a lawsuit, but could unknowingly cause damage to the person, who may be more emotionally disturbed than the analyst realizes.

We itemize eleven specific identifiers representing early fears and anxieties.

Basically, we can assume that emotional disturbances in children are rooted in fears based on insecurities. Everyone has to work through a certain amount of insecurity in her or his life. Generally, everyone has at least two, three, or four fear areas to overcome in a lifetime. Sometimes the analyst will only see the residue of these early fears.

Use a scoring chart from one to seven, (seven being the highest), it would be quite normal to have several fears appear in a script, but scoring on the low side of the chart. (These will be found in the two or three columns of the chart). It is still normal for persons to have one of their fears score high, (in a four or five column) on your chart. The lower the scores are on your 'fear chart,' the more you can assume that the person you are analyzing has worked through their early childhood insecurities.

Remember: A certification in handwriting analysis and the knowledge that you are able to obtain from a script does not meet the qualification of a counselor or psychologist unless you have obtained a degree in these areas.

Graphs on the following page:

Graphs #1 and #2 scores are in a normal range for fear traits.

Graphs #3 and #4 have several low scored fears and one rather high scored fear trait. These are still within the normal range of fear traits.

Graphs #5 and #6 have very high scored fear traits and would be of concern to the analyst. Immediately the analyst should move to the defense columns to see if the personality can sustain and properly cope with such a great amount of fear.

The defense traits as wholesome protectors, resistance (fight) and escape (flight), will be presented after the fear and trauma sections of this chapter.

1. **Desire for attention** is an unfulfilled need for recognition, approval and/ or to be appreciated by others. This can be either real or imagined by the child. When the attention given a child falls short of the child's need, it is natural for the child to try to gain more emotional security. You have already learned that the stroke for this specific indicator is a final upswing at the end of words. When this compensation for unmet needs becomes very strong the finals will grow increasingly larger indicating that the child, now an adult, will play excessively for attention in one way or another.

2. **Self-criticism and blame** may start early in life or come later in life, but it always indicates some type of guilt feelings. The person looks back on some painful event with disapproval. The final stroke in a word also moves back ward but in a stabbing, punishing fashion, often in the crossing of the "t" from right to left. The person may vocalize this displeasure internally or become involved in high risk activities. Basically, this blame is unfounded because it is so often just the result of the human condition. Of course, the weight of the stroke, in this Specific identifier and/or the length of its back-to-self stabbing will indicate its punishing effect.

3. **Indecisiveness** is the fear of finality and causes the person to vacillate between alternatives. It is indicated by

weak, feathering endings and determines the arrange-ment, form, and movement of the writing. This fear trait can be construed to be a form of self-presentation because the person's view of making a decision as an entrapment which offers no escape.

4. **Self-consciousness** more often than not comes from having been put down and ridiculed as a child either in the home or at school. A child must be corrected and guided through life, but if the child is humiliated or made the brunt of jokes because of some "difference," then the child is likely to suffer for many years. This specific indicator can be recognized by the last hump of an "m" or "n" ex-tending higher than the preceding humps. The higher the last hump and the frequency with which it is seen in a writing determines its strength.

5. **Self-underestimation** is the lack of self-esteem which is an essential element for successful living and the ability to reach one's potential. When a child does not receive enough early emotional security s/he will struggle with the fear of failure for years. This Specific indicator can be seen quickly in low "t" bar crossing. In more extreme cases the crossings are below the mid zone letters. Often the analyst will see outstanding talent in a handwriting only to realize that, in the eyes of the individual, this talent is very under-estimated. This, of course, stifles the development of many a gifted person.

6. **Sensitiveness to criticism** is the fear of disapproval re-sulting from repeated hurt or criticism from an early age. A child's greatest need is to be loved and valued. Many children, if not most, hear more criticism from their par-ents and teachers than praise. The specific indicator is a large loop on either the 11d" or the "t" formation. The larger these two loops are, coupled with a lively imagina-

tion (lower zone loops), the greater the impact of this fear trait. Every individual is sensitive to disapproval, but most are able to evaluate the criticism in perspective. The overly sensitive individual will "see" or experience criticism where there may be none, resulting in a feeling of inadequacy.

7. **Rejection** shows that the child fears the loss of affection and/ or status. This is seen in the personal pronoun I." It can indicate poor bonding with one or other of the parents or both. Without the feeling of being accepted, receiving affection or the building of self-worth, there is no bonding and then the child, and later the adult, is like a ship without a rudder. The writer stumbles through life and in and out of one relationship after another. Unfortunately, this Specific identifier is a direct result of the child's perception of the parents. It may not be a true perception of the parenting that actually took place.

8. **Repression** chokes self-expression, buries feelings and cuts off spontaneity. Retraced "m's" and "n's" are the main indicators of this complicated fear. It is complicated because it is so submerged in the unconscious that it is unrecognizable. Even though suppression and repression are in some ways similar they are different. Suppression, as a process, is a conscious and intermittent, holding back of emotional expressions (a squeezed writing form) while repression is an unconscious and constant type of "wiping out" (going over a downstroke with an upstroke) of hurtful memories.

9. **Fear of rivalry** is basically a fear of not being lovable. It consists of comparing oneself with others and coming up short. This can be the result of parent and/ or teacher input or just that the child has taken it upon herself/himself to react in this way.

10 **Withdrawal**, seen in reclined slant, results when a child's spontaneity is stifled or the child experiences some form of rejection and s/he emotionally withdraws. This is a form of protection, writing in a backward slant, signifies repressed emotions so that the child now views life in relation to herself / him self.

11 **Worry** is feeling of distress and/ or anxiety in regard to the present or the future. Seen in extra loops in "the legs" of the "M's" and "N's." It is a sad fact that worry does not change a thing in a person's life.

Trauma may or may not be part of childhood experiences. A trauma occurs after a shattering experience such as a loss of a sibling, loved one or a divorce, to mention a few. Some kind of trauma has occurred when there are split (stenciled looking) letters, twists in letters and/or a general trauma in the handwriting.

Of course, these latter can also indicate a physical, medical and/ or drug related problem, so it is well to speak directly with the person in order to determine with which of these situations you are dealing. The "d" is directly related to **self-feel** and if this is twisted or bent in any fashion, it is a sure sign that the child has experienced some abuse either psychologically or physically. Other signs are soldering, stabs in ovals, and/or under strokes, phallic signs, clothesline garlands, inner bubbles, dark spots, some letters rubbing up against each other and claws.

Defenses

The ego must be protected at all costs. All children and adults seek approval, recognition, and acceptance from their peers. Much emotional energy is exerted defensively to maintain these needs. According to the measure of maturity and security the individual has attained, choices are made about the manner to defend oneself. The major wholesome defenses (adjusters) that we can determine in handwriting analysis are eighteen in number. When these adjusters fail to sustain the ego, the individual will automatically make a choice of either resisting (fight) or escaping (flight) in order to survive.

It is desirable to have high scores in the wholesome ego defenses and low scores in the resistant/escape defenses. Of course, any scores which are abnormally high would be a "red flag" for the analyst and possibly a "stopper" when it comes to realizing an individual's potential, e.g., too much caution would stop a person "dead in their tracks" or too much "humor" might be a facade covering inner conflicts and / or too much philosophical development-a "cop out"-so the analyst must always be vigilant, assessing the whole to determine how secure and mature the individual is.

REMEMBER: One specific identifier which should not be high is perfectionism. As it moves toward a five score there can be genuine problems with the flexibility so necessary for one to move with the flow of life.

Graphs #1 and #2 scores are in a normal range for resistance.
Graphs #3 and #4 scores indicate frustration and, therefore, unhappiness in some area of the writer's life.

RESISTANCE: (Fight) DEFENSES

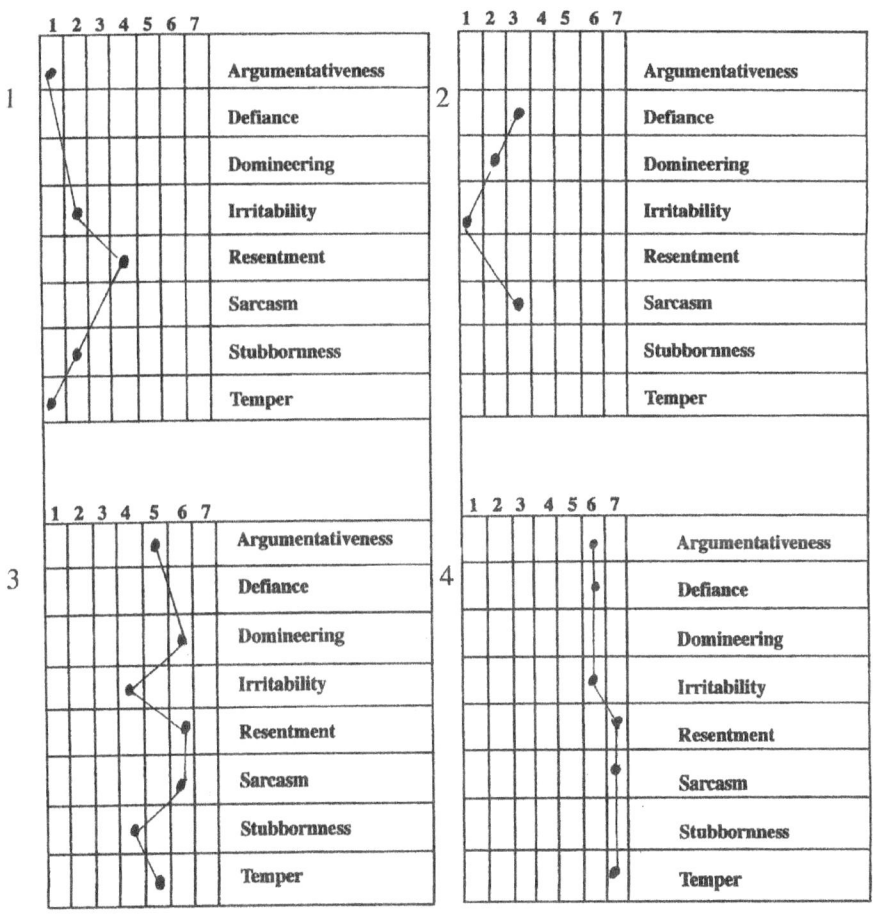

There are Eight Resistance (fight) Defenses that we can identify.

These eight significant identifiers indicate frustration. High scores would indicate intense frustration. The Wholesome Ego Protectors are usually sufficient for a person to maintain emotional balance and to feel secure. If a person finds her/himself in a very unproductive, unsatisfactory, and unhappy situation where there is little recourse or hope and feels backed into a comer, then either the resistance or the escape defenses will take over. Each person has a preference to choose to fight or flee in these situations.

High scores are red flags for the analyst. In a well-balanced writing the fight and flight defenses are few and the scores are low. We all need these back up defenses of fight and flight, but they should be in the background of our personality (two or three of them is normal) but the scores for them should be on the low side of the scale. It is also quite normal for a person to have at least one fairly strong score in both the fight area and the flight area.

At the beginning of this chapter we said that this is the core to any handwriting analysis. This is so not because of the fears presented above nor even the whole some ego defenses also presented above, but because one quick glance at the areas of fight and flight will tell you immediately how secure and mature the person is, how settled, how balanced, and how happy the person is in her / his present situation at home and/ or at work High scores indicate trouble. Low resistance scores are not only desirable but will give you a quick "Happiness Quotient."

It is also true that if the person you are analyzing has not developed many high scored Wholesome Ego Protections there is going to be too strong a reliance on the Resistance and Escape traits and, of course, this will mean that the person does not function well in society and/ or is unable to be peaceful and productive in the work place. So, you see how important it is for you to memorize the Eight Significant Resistance Identifiers and the Thirteen Significant Escape Identifiers.

One of the most important questions an analyst must constantly ask her/ himself is why? Why is this person angry? Why is this person hiding from reality? Why is this person not productive? Why is this person insecure? Why is this person off balance? Why is this person so unhappy and frustrated?

We cannot, as analysts, diagnose problems. However, it helps our analysis to be able to understand where the person has been, what has he/ she overcome and what is causing pain and failure. Certainly, in personnel work we can say very little, but when we work with people one-on-one it is very helpful to be able to compassionately let the person know our findings, along with their strengths and possibilities.

> **Reminder**: All of the specific identifiers in the eight resistance (fight) areas indicate that the writer attacks to defend the self.

1. **Argumentativeness** is generally found in the small "p" formation. It is identified as a point made higher than the buckle of the "p." This point may be made by a straight downward stroke from the UZ or a beginning upward approach stroke. The argumentativeness is intensified if the "p" has a stiff up stroke to it which adds resentment or a deep breakaway stroke which gives it aggressiveness. When we observe a loop on top of the buckle, the writer is a fluid arguer and is gathering more information to present as you are trying to make your point.

Sometimes we see the buckle pulled back into the "p" formation itself as if to hide. This means that the writer is trying to stifle her/ his need to defend the self by arguing. The argumentative writer basically feels that to be wrong is to lose face. There are certainly times when a friendly argument clarifies and defines ideas. What we have in the Significant Identifier of argumentativeness is a resistance trait to justify the writer's position regardless of right or wrong. Constant arguing signals a basic insecurity which, when used as an active resistance, suggests hostility in a greater or lesser degree. depending on other aspects in the writing.

2. **Defiance** can be seen in a writing that has a high "k" buckle that rises above the MZ area. This specific identifier can also be seen in a capital made in the middle or at the end of a word. When the buckle of the "k" rises completely out of the MZ area (action area) and is in the UZ area it may simply represent thoughts of defiance rather than defiance itself. Defiance is a rebellion against authority figures of real or perceived earlier injustices.

The writer may have this Specific identifier but never show it unless the "nerve" that sparked the defiance at an earlier time is pressed upon again. Then the defiant reaction, that others take to be a burst of anger, shows itself for what it is by bringing up all kinds of past injustices unrelated to the present situation. Only by evaluating the whole writing will the analyst know if this is just an "on guard attitude" or an easily activated rebellion in the personality.

3. **Domineering** is indicated by a downward slanted, spurlike "t" bar. The domineering individual is usually called "bossy or demanding" by others. It is a sign that these writers are very frustrated with their own self and/or life. Because these writers cannot get their own personal life in order they try to get other people's lives in order to make

themselves feel better. This is a specific identifier which is a futile means of controlling others and is generally quite overt and easy to ascertain.

Acury provides sampling services tailored to the specific needs of our clients.

2

to make a long story short rasied tim. Children. my kids, Her kids and or Kids till my Kid, your Kids and or Kid to be great.

3

Perhaps they feel uncomfortable having woman as their team, but I am too content leading them and not being accepted as one of their peers.

4. **Irritability** can be seen by "i" and "j" dots that are made with stabbing motions. When the jabbing motion is pointed to the left it is likely that the writer is unhappy with her/himself. When the jabbing motions are pointed toward the right, it is more likely that this is directed at others. This is a milder resentment-specific identifier than the others, but it can be quite unpleasant. It may mean that the writer is

over involved, pushing her / himself too hard or is in an unpleasant situation at home or at work.

4   *I am writing in regard*

5   *he leadeth me beside the*

6   *I love to travel*

7   *that the writing is a litt*

8   *this coming Wednesday*

5. **Resentment** when very strong, can easily be picked up by the analyst by running the eyes down the left margin.

This specific identifier shows stiff up strokes at the beginning of many or all words in the text. When these stiff up strokes come from below the line of writing they are indicative of deep surging resentment and the writer is likely to be "touchy."

All of these stiff upstrokes indicate that the writer's guards are up against being unjustly imposed upon. This imposition may be real or imagined in the writer's mind. Certainly, this trait began with someone taking advantage of the writer somewhere along the line, but now, when the stroke is consistent in the writing, the writer views all persons as perched to take advantage of her I him at any moment.

6. **Sarcasm** can be seen by the sharp point at the end of a "t" bar crossing. Generally, the writer who makes this specific indicator unconsciously wants to punish the recipient of the barbed remark out of her I his own feelings of inadequacy.

The "sting" is an offensive form of protection and a way of belittling the other person in order to bring her / him down to the writer's level. However, it is well to realize that sarcasm can be used both defensively or offensively. When there are no other high scored resistant traits the analyst can assume that the sarcasm seen in the writing is merely there to protect and is not necessarily activated often.

7. **Stubbornness** is a "tent" formation primarily under the letters "t" and "d" and in some "m's" and "n's." This specific identifier must have a "braced look" to qualify as stubbornness. When stubbornness is used as a resistance trait, it indicates a refusal to yield, even in the face of reason. It is a face saving measure to protect the ego by refusing to admit that there may be a mistake in judgment.

8. **Temper** can primarily be seen when a "t" bar is made to the right of the "t" stem. The stroke is not grounded but free flowing because it has missed its mark. Some of these temper strokes are in the form of a "tick" in that they are a quick angle attached to a capital letter. These specific indicators rep resenting temper and frustration are signs of a tendency toward underlying temper by an angry person habitually on the alert.

A word about anger in particular and controllers in general: Anger can reside in strange places and its sister, "control", has many faces. A person can control by sickness, by needing special foods, by tears, by being late, by putting things off, by incessant talking or laughing. These are not always easy for an analyst to pick up quickly in the writing, but these often become evident in a one-on-one hand writing evaluation session. Every analyst should read about anger and its many faces. Once one of the "faces" is seen, try to find its mark in the script.

ESCAPE: (flight) DEFENSES

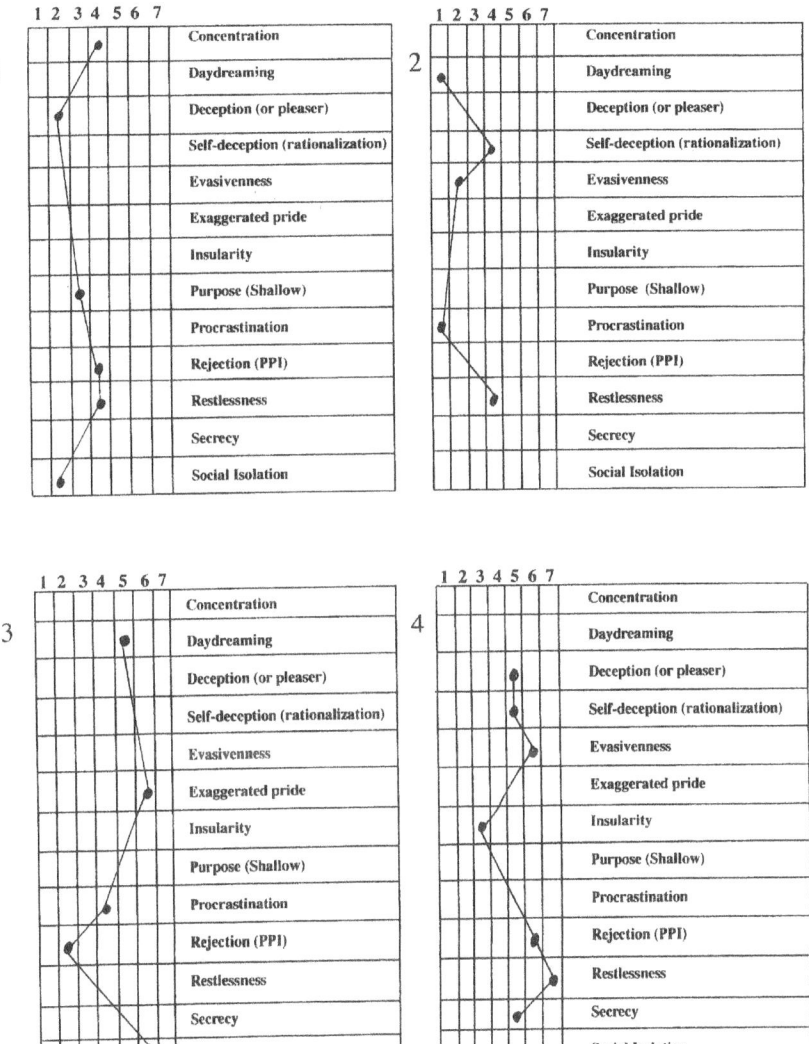

Graphs #1 and #2 scores are in a normal range for escapes. Graphs #3 and #4 scores indicate hiding from reality and are a concern.

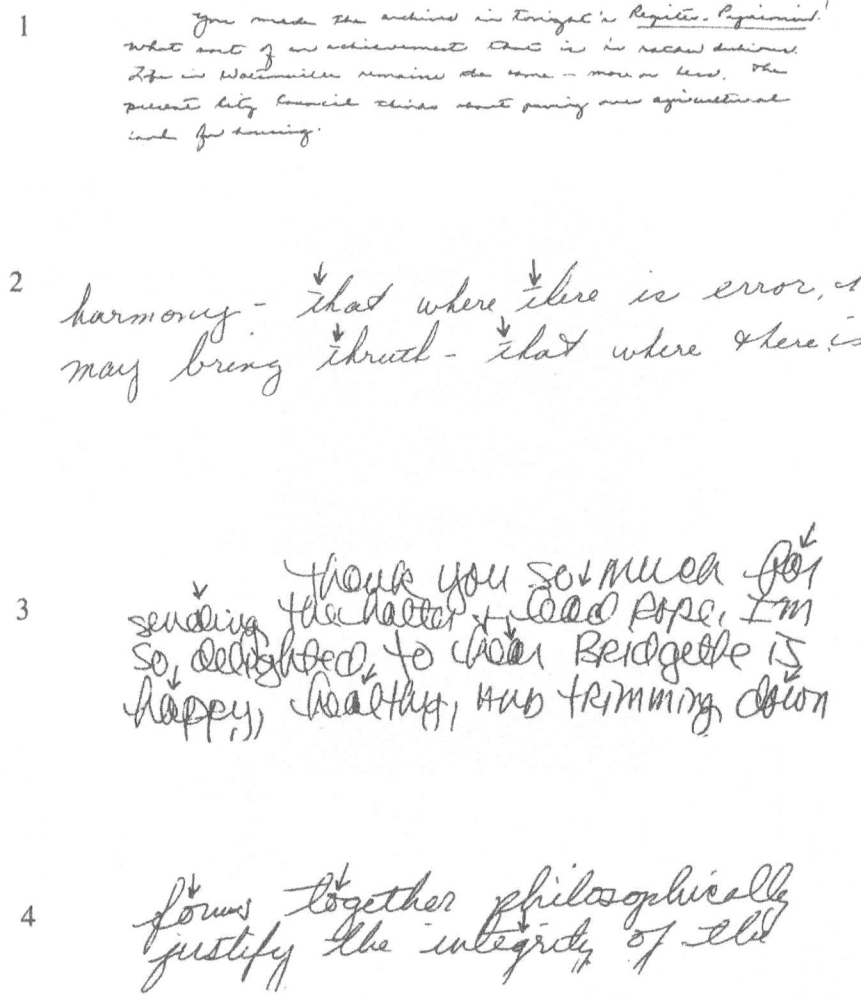

ESCAPE: (Flight) DEFENSES

There are Twelve Escapes (flight) that we can identify.

As we have said above, the ego must be protected at all costs. If the wholesome ego adjusters break down and the individual is not inclined to fight for her/ his rights then it becomes imperative that the individual escape from the pain of reality by using denial. As Scott Peck mentions in his book, *The Road Less Traveled*, it is more painful in the long run to avoid difficulties than it is to face them right away.

In our discussion of fears, anxiety, and trauma we pointed out that these defensive forces affect our lives in various ways. We tend to build up our defenses one after another without even realizing that we are doing so. Here the analyst's ability to help another see these defensive drives which change a personality and realize that he/ she does not need to go to such great lengths to solve problems will help to stabilize a fearful personality.

Many adults do not realize that their self-esteem is at a low ebb because they have formed a low opinion of themselves, their abilities, their gifts. Not daring to aspire to their optimum gifts puts them in the unenviable position of turning to the opinions of others to learn about themselves.

Creating an idealized image of themselves only leads to more injury. They spend their time being hostile to those who seem to have gifts they lack, avoiding anyone who, in their opinion, is superior to them in some way. This leads them to ignore their creative abilities, and innate attractiveness as they step back and take refuge in isolation and pretended dignity.

Fear usually proceeds from conflicts people have not been able to resolve. The compassionate analyst can guide them to personality integration through suggesting that they solve their problems in a more secure and mature fashion.

1. **Concentration** is easily ascertained by looking and measuring the MZ; concentration is necessary for each of us in a greater or lesser degree, but when concentration is

used as an escape, it is focused on the self to the exclusion of all else. This can cause emotional problems. If the MZ measurement is less than 1/16 it is important to evaluate how healthy the person is in regard to the wholesome ego protectors indicated. Adjusters showing high scores and resistance and escapes having low scores depicts a secure person.

2. **Daydreaming** when the "t" bar floats above the "t" stem the writer's goals are unconnected to reality. What better way to escape from painful reality of what might have been, than to dream of all that might someday be by building castles in the air?

3. **Deception** is indicated by two inner loops on an "a," "o," or a "d." When these inner loops are large there is more chance that the person just wants to be accepted and will say whatever it takes to make this happen. While this certainly is a form of lying, it is not as serious as when the inner two loops are very small and tightly made into a "bow tie" effect. This type of deceit is more insidious because it is more intentional.

Deceit is a result of fear, the fear of being exposed as not smart enough, good enough or worthy of another's love and respect. As an escape it points to insecurity, even if it is a bad habit left over from childhood, it is self-defeating and lowers all other character scores. When working one-on-one with a client it is possible for the analyst to point out, compassionately, how unnecessary this trait is in relation to the total personality and the writer's potential.

4. **Self-deception** — rationalization is identified as having an inner left loop within a circle letter, "a," "o," "d," or "g." The deception is not projected outward toward another but inward toward the self. It is the self that is deceived. The

writer unconsciously covers over some of the facts of a situation by denying that she/ he had any part in it at all.

It is important to note that the person does not intend to deceive others but only to deceive the self. It is just too painful for the individual to admit some blame in a given situation. Most people recognize when a person is using this escape mechanism. It takes a great deal of security to own up to one's part in a failed situation.

5. **Evasiveness** made with an inner loop that moves along with and "hugs" the initial loop of the "a" formation. It is a protective procedure that comes from insecurity and a method of side stepping reality because of real or perceived pain.

6. **Exaggerated** pride appears generally in "t's" and "d's" that are excessively tall for the script. It can also be indicated in any of the UZ letters that appear excessively elongated. Exaggerated pride signifies an extreme need for approval coming from feelings of inferiority. Since the writer does not experience approval from others, s/he compensates for this real or imagined disapproval by exaggerated self-approval.

Some who have this specific identifier have had lonely childhoods where they have had to go into their heads for mental approval. The result is that now he or she puts on an air of superiority which makes it hard for others to relate to him or her. Often these writers will sell themselves higher than they are able to produce

7. **Insularity** seen by the analyst as very small, tight loop formations at the end of the LZ. Since the return of the LZ loop indicates fulfilling relationships, these truncated LZ loops signify unsuccessful personal and social relationships. The writer who has tried and failed in relationships over and over again, will begin to withdraw into the self to

protect the ego resulting in an unhealthy situation. Professional help should be recommended, depending on the amount and the intensity of these small LZ loops.

5

[handwritten sample]

6

response to my request for information. would "like" to try your "drop-in hour," as it

7

maybe? In reviewing the evaluation and pondering the past, one thing did pop out: Until age two, my family

8

Old paint on canvas, as it ages, sometimes becomes transparent. When that happens it is possible, in some pictures, to see the original lines: a tree will show through, a woman

8. **Purpose** (shallow) is represented by a "dish-like" cross bar on a "t" formation. This "caved in crossing" indicates one form of directional pressure. The "dish-like" crossing must be seen on a free standing "t" to qualify, not on a fluid "t" moving into an "h" formation.

Because the cross bar is "caved in" the pressure is coming from above and indicates a writer as having experienced someone more powerful than her / himself pressuring the person into submission. Now, if writer is in another like situation she/ he may quickly leave, deserting a job or a relationship. Some analysts define this as "shallow," which has some merit, but actually it can be seen as a "wound" that acts as an emotional escape when undue pressure is experienced again in the person's life. This does translate as a risk factor in a personal or personnel situation.

9. **Procrastination** can be found when a "t" bar does not reach the place of crossing the stem. A writer who makes this type of delayed "t" crossing is procrastinating because of fear; the fear of not doing the work satisfactorily, the fear of being criticized after the work is completed, or some other fear of being ridiculed which is generally unfounded.

10. **Restlessness** can be quickly seen by examining the LZ of a writing sample. This restless stroke is a prolonged downward thrust of a "y" or "g." This significant identifier is essentially one of constantly being on the move, (after all one can't hit a moving target), unconsciously desiring to run away from a painful situation.

11. **Secrecy** is shown by a final tied loop made on the right side of an "a" or an "o" formation. Secretiveness is a conscious desire to withhold information for one reason or another. The writer does not try to deceive or mislead but just withholds information. This is because she/ he realizes that there are problems, but does not feel it is necessary to share them. Generally, the problems are of a personal nature and happily, as the writer works these problems, the secretive loop disappears from the writing.

The strength of this Significant Identifier de pends on the frequency of the stroke and the size of the loop.

9   *I like to make more*

10   *Thank you very much for taking the time to look at my Handwriting and tell me what it says.*

11   *I really enjoy the work, enjoy working with people. Learning new things, keeping busy. I feel I have a good attitude about dental health,*

12   *I am working on the meditation and am curious to see what it will bring. Although it doesn't seem probable that I'll be able to take the classes*

12. **Social isolation** spacing is determined by large word or line spacing in the writing. When the word spacing is larger than average, the writer finds too much contact distressing and has difficulty communicating. When the line spacing is larger than average, the need for privacy is even more pronounced. Social isolation, being a fear of close contact, is a protection against the pain that social contacts inevitably cause every individual from time to time. **REMEMBER**: All twelve specific identifiers in this area mean that the writer will avoid reality to defend the self.

When we find persons who come to us trapped in feelings of fear and inadequacy, we have the ability to calm them, and help them recognize the "why" of the early painful situations in their lives. We can then point out the many adjustment defenses that they have which protect them from harm. We can assure them that they have survived very well in the past, and suggest what to use for help in their future.

Working with persons *trapped in feelings of frustration,* we will be able to ask them just how happy they are in their present situations. We can then help them to realize that attacking, to defend themselves, creates more problems than it solves.

When we see persons *who are running from reality,* we are able to explain the fact that they are just postponing the inevitable and prolonging the pain. Scott Peck points out in his book *The Road Less Traveled,* that one of the great truths is that life is difficult! Once we come to this realization, we have the ability to transcend it. "Life is a series of problems;" "Do we want to moan about them or solve them?"

We all try to avoid rather than face pain. Unfortunately, if we use substitutes such as attacking and escaping "the substitute itself ultimately becomes more painful than the legitimate suffering it was designed to avoid."

> **Remember**: *Attacking and escaping, when in the high score range, are areas where the balance and the emotional health of the person can be measured. Excessive use of either attack or escape, alerts the analyst to the fact the person needs professional help. It is well, for the analyst, to have the business cards of reputable counselors and psychologists ready to hand out.*

In closing, let us not forget that fear is not a reality—only love is a reality. Ruth Holmes once pointed out in one of her presentations that the letters that make up the word FEAR stand for False Evidence Appearing Real.

> **Monk**: *I understand that when a lion seizes upon his opponent, whether it is a hare or an elephant, he makes an exhaustive use of his power; pray tell me what is this power?*

> **Master**: *The spirit of sincerity (literally, the power of 'not deceiving').*

Sincerity—that is, not-deceiving—means "putting forth one's whole being," technically known as "the whole being in action" ... in which nothing is kept in reserve, nothing is expressed under disguise, nothing goes to waste. When a person lives like this, he is said to be a golden-haired lion; he is the symbol of virility, sincerity, wholeheartedness; he is divinely human.

DT. Suziki, Zen Buddhism and Its Influence on Japanese Culture, The Eastern Buddhist Society (Kyoto), 1938.

Your Temperament is Showing

INTRODUCTION

One of the most fascinating subjects to deal with is personality. It is important to understand each others personality types if we are to attempt communication in a pleasant, humane manner. Our mental, spiritual, emotional, and physical differences, while adding the uniqueness that separates us from every other individual, can lead to incompatibilities in relationships which seem insurmountable.

However, if we take time to study individual personalities, we will discover that we are often attracted to a person with a personality totally different from ours. Understanding these differing personality types will enable us to solve many communication problems that otherwise create misunderstanding and pain.

It is for this reason that *Your Temperament Is Showing In Your Handwriting* is being presented. The authors hope that it will prove to be yet another tool for the graphoanalyst in helping others to cope with—even to enjoy—the differences each unique individual presents.

Studying personality types is not a new science. It takes us back some 2000 years ago to Afghanistan with the oral tradition of the Sufi masters who identified nine types of personality in a system they called the Enneagram, taken from the Greek word "enneas" or nine. Later the study of personality differences and temperamental characteristics by Hippocrates (460-370 B.C.) gave us the four temperament types choleric, sanguine, melancholic, and phlegmatic. It is these four types and the blends that result from them, identified by Hippocrates and used extensively in personality studies from his time to the present, that we are considering here.

A most reliable way to understand oneself and others is to study the temperaments. Knowing one's temperament will help a person to develop the positive traits and gradually improve the less positive, while the ability to discover and understand individual temperaments makes it possible to direct, guide, and educate another. This skill is of the utmost importance for educators, administrators, parents, and professionals of all types.

Consideration of reactions to the same experience by different individuals shows these reactions to be different with each personality type.

Sanguine reaction is instant but of weak duration; the choleric reacts immediately and the strong reaction endures. The melancholic, on the other hand, does not usually give exterior signs of reaction, but in the process of internalizing the event develops a deep and lasting reaction. The phlegmatic person is only slightly excited by impressions received, so does not react immediately, if at all, and the impression is not lasting. From the varying reaction of different persons to the same stimuli, we determine temperament types.

Observing reactions in situations, such as, when a person is complimented, criticized, insulted, feeling sympathetic to another, enlisting in a cause, experiencing dislike toward someone or faced with a danger, we arrive at a degree of accuracy in determining the temperament types.

Of the four main types, the choleric and sanguine are outer-directed (extroverted) and active, while the melancholic and phlegmatic are inner directed (introverted) and passive, preferring a quiet approach to life.

Outer-directed, the strong-willed choleric seeks involvement, great success in business, top positions—especially in management—and enjoy the challenge of overcoming difficulties. The outer-directed, restless sanguine loves the social life, public relations, the limelight, and get energy from being with others, especially if the encounter involves bringing enjoyment to others.

The inner-directed, gifted melancholics react in a more reserved, consistent manner and can be found in endeavors that call for self-sacrifice, idealism, and service. Most comfortable watching the involvement of others, the calm, easygoing, introverted phlegmatic is not easily swayed by emotions. Most at home in detail jobs, such as computer work, statistics, and microscopic examinations, the phlegmatic is a very capable, intelligent individual who appreciates the arts.

Scarcely anyone exhibits the qualities of only one temperament. Most of us are a blend, that is, one temperament predominates, while another is also evident. In some cases, two temperaments are so mixed that both are equally strong. It is often difficult for people to determine their own particular temperament, while it is easier for us to notice the characteristics in another.

It is hoped that a careful study of the characteristics, handwriting traits, reactions, manners and expressions of others will not only help us understand them better, excuse them more often, cherish their good traits, overlook their less-pleasing traits, but will also lead to a greater knowledge of ourselves and others—why we act and react as we do.

It is well for us to remember that we are born with our temperaments and although we might like to do so, we are not able to make an exchange for one we like better. Our task is to develop and cultivate all of the good traits in our temperament, while overcoming the traits that do not help us to achieve our goals. Knowing our own temperament and understanding the drives and impulses that motivate others will set us on a path of understanding, tolerance, and contentment. It w iii also help us in determining what vocational opportunities to select in order to live life fully and with a high degree of satisfaction.

Not least of all, it will go far toward bringing happiness not only to us individually, but also to those with whom we live and work. Since each temperament is good in itself, we need to accept our own, while seeking out people of differing temperaments for a support and complement to enhance our strengths and supplement our lacks. This is what community, family life, and peaceful living in the global world are all about.

CHAPTER ONE

What Energizes/Motivates/Drives Each Type?

An understanding of personality may well begin with determining what energizes a person. Does energy come from the world without or from the resources within one's own mind? The extrovert is energized through contact with people and with the outside world. Stimulation comes from the surrounding people and things in the environment. Interruptions, especially from the telephone, are not a problem to the extrovert who loves to have people around and is noted for the ability to communicate well.

Extroverts want to make changes that are immediately evident to the world around them. They want to confront this outside world and get involved. The only way they can understand the world and people around them is to talk; so, they talk non-stop. While they are talking they come to an understanding of what they are observing and thinking. They prefer to work with others on a team, finding periods of quiet and solitude very de-energizing. They need sociability, action, and variety.

True introverts, on the other hand, work best in a quiet, uninterrupted environment, and dislike anything that tends to intrude upon their inner world of ideas and understanding. They seek to understand the world about them through concentrated time alone, conceptualizing everything before they act. They usually have some difficulty communicating with others. Long periods of time, surrounded by many people, are very draining to the introvert who needs privacy and quiet to be energized. The introvert can spend hours on a project, thinking, writing, philosophizing, checking each detail to be certain all is perfect.

General Characteristics of Each Temperament

CHOLERIC:Outer-directed (extroverted), more intense than sanguine.

Symbol: ELEPHANT—thick skinned, capable of destroying when angry, powerful.

ASSETS: Productive (ambitious) BORN TO RULE (leader) Aggressive, ambitious, confident, courageous, decisive, determined, dynamic, enduring, energetic, enthusiastic, independent, optimistic, practical, productive, strong-willed.

SHADOW SIDE: Difficult to live with. Hot tempered—anger can degenerate into hatred, revenge, and injustice. Inclined to be arrogant, devious, domineering, egocentric, impetuous, intolerant, obstinate, proud, willful, even cruel. Unappreciative of the arts, but fascinated by utilitarian values.

The least developed part of this temperament is the emotional, so the elephant can be an inconsiderate, self-sufficient and opportunist, lacking in compassion and sympathy. Details are a bore. The choleric is not given to lengthy analysis, but makes quick, intuitive decisions.

BRIGHT SIDE: Sharp intellect, enthusiasm for the noble and great, resolute will, keen vivacity which influences all his/her thoughts and plans.

MOTTO: "I can do it myself!"

Thumbnail Sketch of Strengths: keen intellect, energetic, hot, quick, active, practical, strong-willed, self-sufficient, independent, dynamic, decisive, opinionated, quick decision maker, thrives on activity, stimulates environment with endless ideas, plans immediate and long-range, ambitious, not vacillating under pressure of others' opinions, takes definite stands on issues, can be found crusading for social cause, not frightened by adversity, doggedly determined, succeeds where others fail; keeps on pushing when others quit.

BODY TYPE: Mesomorph (athletic, muscular)

VOCATIONAL CHOICE: Best suited as adventurer, builder, entrepreneur, executive, lawyer, organizer, politician, producer, surgeon

How To Deal With Cholerics:

▷ Train them to apply their good talents to the best advantage.

▷ Make reasonable suggestions to them.

▷ Never try to "break" the obstinate behavior of the choleric—try to lead rather than to push.

▷ Remain calm, allowing them time   to cool off after an explosion.

▷ Persuade them to accept guidance and help in order to minimize faults and to bring out the good qualities they have in abundance.

▷ Appeal to their good will and sense of honor.

▷ Praise their efforts at self-control in order to bring out the positive side of this strong temperament.

SANGUINE: Outer-directed (extroverted), gentle and happy.

Symbol: BUTTERFLY--restless, frivolous, expansive, beautiful, and colorful, flying from flower to flower.

ASSETS: Personality (carefree) BORN TO PLEASE (entertainer and friend) Carefree, cheerful, contented, empathetic, enthusiastic, friendly, humorous, kindly, optimistic, outgoing, people-oriented, personable, popular, sociable, spontaneous, talented.

SHADOW SIDE: Careless, distracted, easily influenced by praise and flattery, egocentric, emotional, gossipy, impractical, inconsistent, intemperate, irresolute, irresponsible, moody, restless, scattered, sensual, superficial, undisciplined, unstable, vain. Emotions, rather than reflective thought, are the basis of most decisions.

BRIGHT SIDE: Communicative, friendly, pleasant, obliging, compassionate, cheerful, forgiving, docile, candid, dramatic story teller, naturally receptive, warm and friendly, life of the party, compliant, optimistic, never at a loss for words, loves variety, exciting, gets along well with difficult people.

MOTTO: "Let's try it!"

Thumbnail Sketch of Strengths: Disarming sincerity, exciting, pleasant and willing to oblige, compassionate and always ready to cheer others, seldom shows resentment, bears no grudge, does not worry for long about failure, optimistic.

BODY TYPE: Endomorph (soft, round, plump)

VOCATIONAL CHOICE: Best suited as entertainer, cruise director, flight attendant, salesperson, instructor, outside work, personal service, popular arts, receptionist, nurse.

How To Deal With Sanguines:

▷ Furnish strict supervision and guidance.

▷ Insist that they finish their work.

▷ Check up continually on their work.

▷ Think twice before taking them into your confidence.

▷ Accept their cheerfulness and let them have their fun, but guard them against overdoing it.

MELANCHOLIC: Inner-directed (introvert), intense thinker.

Symbol: FROG—characterized by intense concentration, darting looks, and a quick tongue.

ASSETS: Perfectionist, humanitarian, promoter. Aesthetic, altruistic, analytical, cause-oriented, conscientious, creative, gentle, gifted, idealistic, intense, loyal, persevering, quick, reflective, reserved, self-sacrificing, sensitive, serious, soft-hearted, understanding, zealous

SHADOW SIDE: Anxious, critical, dependent, despondent, emotional, envious, irresolute, moody, nit-picking, passive, pessimistic, procrastinating, retiring, revengeful, rigid, self -centered, sensitive, suspicious, theoretical, unsociable, worried.

BRIGHT SIDE: Thoughtful, careful worker, industrious, caring, loyal, logical, serious, highly energetic, competitor.

MOTTO: "It won't work!"

Thumbnail Sketch Of Strengths: Ability to internalize with ease and joy. Not preoccupied with material things to the exclusion of the needs of others. Finds deep thought restful and productive. Often is a great benefactor to others. Good counselor in difficulties; is a prudent, trustworthy, well-meaning friend. Has great sympathy with others and a great desire to make sacrifices to help them.

BODY TYPE: Ectomorph (linear, tense, nervous)

VOCATIONAL CHOICE: Best suited to be caregiver, educator, fine arts, health service, humanitarian, inventor, minister, musician, poet, preacher, reformer, searcher, social service worker.

How To Deal With Melancholics:

▷ Always show sympathy and understanding.

▷ Gain their confidence by showing unselfish love for them.

▷ Always give encouragement. (Friendly advice and patience will work wonders.)

▷ Do not overburden them with work, but keep them busy.

▷ Remember that melancholics are very sensitive and treat them accordingly.

▷ Give necessary punishment with precaution and kindness, avoiding any appearance of injustice.

PHLEGMATIC: Inner-directed (introverted), gentle, relaxed.

Symbol: Turtle—relaxed, calm, solid, slow.

ASSETS: Persistence—retentive mind (Thinker). Amiable, calm, cautious, dependable, diplomatic, easy-going, efficient, empathetic, humorous, peaceable, practical, prudent, thorough, tolerant, wise.

SHADOW SIDE: Unmotivated, conservative, inflexible, critical, distrustful, procrastinating, selfish, shy, withdrawn, stubborn, lacks energy, indecisive and fearful, careless, and easy-going, stingy, self-protective, selfish.

BRIGHT SIDE: Natural for detailed work, neat, efficient and organized in work habits, sees the comic in life and others, spectator personality, kind-hearted and sympathetic, peace-maker.

MOTTO: "Today?"

Thumbnail Sketch of Strengths: Possesses a rare sense of humor; has a retentive mind, and is a natural for detailed work; likes to tease in a non-threatening way; appreciates difficulties of others; has a charming, conciliatory effect on others; is not easily offended; remains composed, thoughtful, deliberate, sober and practical; works well with children, tolerating their moods; is consistent in discipline.

BODY TYPE: Endomorph--soft, round, overweight.

VOCATIONAL CHOICE: Accountant, computer analyst, counselor, diplomat, inventor, librarian, nurse, philosopher, psychologist, researcher, scientist, teacher, technician, therapist.

How To Deal With Phlegmatics:

▷ Encourage them to set reasonable goals and to follow a well-planned rule of life.

▷ Help them to overcome their passivity through involvement with others.

▷ Get them involved in community work, giving up their spectator role and forgetting their own selfish needs.

▷ Convince them by word and example that they are highly intelligent, capable, lovable people with great talent that needs to be cultivated and shared.

▷ Bring them to realize that their stubbornness and foot-dragging are hindrances not only to their own progress but that of others.

▷ Find ways to help them face their problems rather than ignoring them, making it clear that "peace at any price" only brings greater problems.

CHAPTER TWO

Discovering Temperament In Handwriting

Every handwriting analyst who is serious about helping others to understand themselves will want to explore any available avenue that opens to new ways of testing human reaction in terms of personality traits as well as the know ledge of the basic emotions, mental processes, motivations, fears, defenses, social traits, and aptitudes.

As an aid to personal counseling, vocational guidance, job placement, and ways for individuals to discover and understand the facet s of their personalities which make them react in a particular manner, a knowledge of temperament is invaluable in helping the analyst point out the strengths which spell success for a client, as well as the drawbacks which tend to hinder progress.

Personality includes all of the qualities and characteristics which a person possesses. The patterns of behavior or moral nature ofindividuals make up their character. Temperament, on the other hand, is the sum total of inherited traits, combined with our acquired psychological, social, and ethical traits, that subconsciously influence us in everything we do.

To discover our potential, we need to know the basic temperament and character traits which are unique to each of us as an individual. A good handwriting analyst will not be satisfied with merely naming traits that are found in the handwriting, but will also wish to understand them in relation to the personality, character, and temperament in order to get a total picture of the client.

Although we can list extroverts, introverts and ambiverts, describing characteristics which identify each, we always need to be aware that it would be unusual to find any one person who fits perfectly into any one description. We can, however, list enough general traits and characteristics to make it possible to show how each individual falls into one or two general patterns of temperament.

Rev. Norman Werling, the graphoanalyst par excellence, has done significant study over the years to show the correlation between handwriting and temperament. In brief he lists tempo, pressure, letter pattern, height, width, and zone sizes as most significant indicators. Giving a graphic, humorous visual help. Father Werling identifies the temperaments through the symbols of the elephant, butterfly, frog, and turtles. A paraphrase of his descriptions follows.

Choleric: the elephant, a powerful extrovert, is the symbol of strength, physical and moral courage, unlimited energy, power, achievement, and activity. When enraged, the elephant is capable of unbelievable destruction. It has a strong herd instinct, yet frequently goes its own way. There have been remarkable instances of an elephant getting revenge many years after it had been hurt. When properly trained, the elephant can accomplish great feats of work and strength.

Our thoughts and our acts

Create our world!

Sanguine: the butterfly, a gentle extrovert, is the symbol of beauty, restless activity, and fragile existence. Words to describe a butterfly temperament include: cheerful, easy communication, cooperation, optimism, lack of concentration, and physical good looks. Within the species there is a great variety of colors and forms and sizes, but all have the basic characteristics. Butterflies are valuable for the service of transferring pollen, which gives their life meaning beyond their own existence.

I certainly appreciate your analyzing handwriting. As I write this

Melancholic: the frog, a powerful introvert, is a lonely creature, impulsive in its movements; not particularly attractive in its appearance or its croaking, yet equally adapted to land and water. Survival depends on an all-seeing eye and a quick tongue. This temperament is best described as intense, detailed, analytical, perfectionist, and idealistic.

I have enclosed two small samples of each, and it is important that I obtain the

Phlegmatic: the turtles, gentle introverts, are slow-moving creatures, cautious, gentle, quiet, solitary, making their way when they are unafraid and withdrawing into their shells when threatened. The easy tempo of their vitality prolongs their life to great age; just watching them is a lesson in relaxation and the goals that can be achieved just by steady persistence. Best words to describe this temperament are: calm, patient, loyal, persistent, low energy.

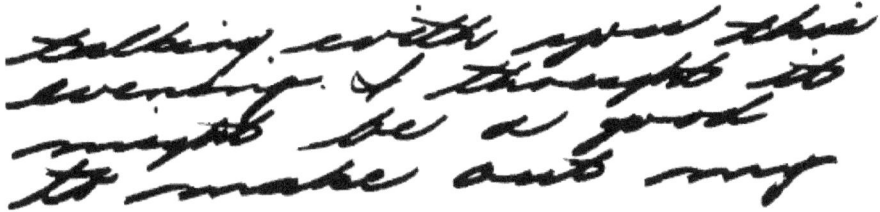

Choleric and sanguine individuals are outer-directed or extroverts, while the melancholic and phlegmatic are inner-directed or introverts. Identifying an individual as extrovert or introvert is another way to determine personality.

On the next page you will find a quick review of the four temperaments in an easy to understand chart, followed by a list of the different blends of types.

A QUICK REVIEW OF THE FOUR TEMPERAMENTS

Symbol:	Elephant Power/strength destruction	Butterfly Beauty/rest- lessness	Frog Loneliness/impul- sive movement	Turtle Relaxed/soli- tary
Type	Extrovert	Extrovert	Introvert	Introvert
Motto:	"Can do it!"	"Try it!"	"It won't work."	"Today?"
Asset:	Ambition	Personality	Cerebral	Persistence
Liability:	Domineering	Restless	Judgmental	Low energy
Orientation To Others:	Competitor Leader	Friend Entertainer	Humanitarian Promoter	Thinker Inventor
Will Power:	Strong	Changeable	Intense	Brief
Intelligence:	Deep/quick	Surface/quick	Logical/slow	Solid/slow
Tempo:	Restless	Spontaneous	Repressed	Slow
Emotions:	External Strong/quick Enduring	External Weak/quick Brief	Internal Strong/deep Rehashed	Internal Light/slow Repressed
Energy:	Strong/ Restless	Moderate/ Enthusiastic	Repressed/ Enduring	Moderate/Low Inflexible
Motivation:	Seeks power	Seeks Recog- nition	Seeks mental pursuit	Seeks peaceful environment
Competition:	High	Attention Seeker	Envious Competitor	Low
Work Habits:	Workaholic	Jack/Jill of all trades	Perfectionist	Routine/ Thorough
Interpersonal:	Against people	Toward people	From people	Above people
Self-esteem:	Superstar	Exaggerated	Needs praise	Low
Characteristic	Dynamic	Cheerful	Serious	Calm
Purpose:	Enduring	Changeable	Intense	Brief

Physique: ▽ Mesomorph ⬤ Endomorph ▢ Ectomorph ⬤ Endomorph

TEMPERAMENT BLENDS

CHOLERIC

SANGUINE

Strengths	Weaknesses	Strengths	Weaknesses
AGGRESSIVE	ANGRY	CHEERFUL	CARELESS
AMBITIOUS	ARROGANT	CONTENTED	DISTRACTED
CONFIDENT	DEVIOUS	EMPATHETIC	GOSSIPY
COURAGEOUS	DOMINEERING	ENTHUSIASTIC	IMPRACTICAL
DECISIVE	EGO-CENTRIC	FRIENDLY	INTEMPERATE
DETERMINED	IMPULSIVE	HUMOROUS	IRRESOLUTE
DYNAMIC	INCONSIDERATE	KINDLY	IRRESPONSIBLE
ENDURING	INTOLERANT	OPTIMISTIC	MOODY
ENERGETIC	OBSTINATE	OUTGOING	RESTLESS
ENTHUSIASTIC	PROUD	PEOPLE-ORIENTED	SCATTERED
INDEPENDENT	REVENGEFUL	PERSONABLE	SENSUAL
OPTIMISTIC	SARCASTIC	POPULAR	SUPERFICIAL
PRACTICAL	SELF-SUFFICIENT	SOCIABLE	UNDISCIPLINED
PRODUCTIVE	UNSYMPATHETIC	SPONTANEOUS	UNSTABLE
STRONG-WILLED	WILLFUL	TALENTED	VAIN

MELANCHOLY

PHLEGMATIC

Strengths	Weaknesses	Strengths	Weaknesses
AESTHETIC	ANXIOUS	AMIABLE	CONSERVATIVE
ALTRUISTIC	CRITICAL	CALM	CRITICAL
ANALYTICAL	DEPENDENT	CAUTIOUS	DISTRUSTFUL
CONSCIENTIOUS	EMOTIONAL	DEPENDABLE	IMPULSIVE
CREATIVE	ENVIOUS	DIPLOMATIC	INDECISIVE
GENTLE	MOODY	EASY-GOING	LETHARGIC
GIFTED	NIT-PICKING	EFFICIENT	OBSERVING
IDEALISTIC	PESSIMISTIC	EMPATHETIC	PROCRASTINATING
INTENSE	RIGID	HUMOROUS	SELF-PROTECTIVE
LOYAL	SELF-CENTERED	PEACEABLE	SELFISH
PERSEVERING	SENSITIVE	PRACTICAL	SHY
QUICK	SUSPICIOUS	PRUDENT	SLOW
SERIOUS	THEORETICAL	THOROUGH	STUBBORN
UNDERSTANDING	UNSOCIABLE	TOLERANT	TIMID
ZEALOUS	WORRIED	WISE	WITHDRAWN

Process to Determine Main Temperament

The following 12 determinations will help to identify the primary temperament.

1. Gestalt (overview of the handwriting) — Fr. Werling Seminar, 1983

Choleric - Dynamic/Vital

We are all looking forward to your Future visits and Fear that there is a

Sanguine - Restless/Expansive

presuming my response is enough for your study.

Melancholic - Intense/Repressed

How much sleep will I lose tonight worrying about this unexpected incursion into the psyche? Its not just any psyche

Phlegmatic - Relaxed/Soft

I don't have the what to write. this is what everyone however, here it is —

2. MEASURE SLANT

Usually the slant falls in these areas: (Fr. N. Werling)

Choleric–BC-E+

art form + intellect

playing is totally gone.

Sanguine–BC-E

Can you tell me what you see

**Melancholic–
CD-E+**

*I have been inter
nine years now. For
I lived in new york*

Phlegmatic-FA-BC

feel one when I've put an

& variable

3. PRESSURE — (force + pen)

Note: Pressure, being a highly complex topic, is a booklet in itself; so, for this material we will use very simple, direct explanations and refer you to our bibliography of those who are masters in the subject.

Definition: Pressure is the graphological term for equating the force exerted, relative pastosity and sharpness of the inking pattern of the pen on the paper. The different degrees force people apply to their pen or pencil on the writing surface indicates their energy for work or for goal-directed pursuits as they accept or resist their environment.

In general, graphoanalysts measure mental force in the writer's personality as it is observed not only through the pressure exerted but also by the very choice of pen/pencil. Heavy writers generally choose broad-tipped pens or soft-leaded pencils, whereas the light writer prefers a fine point and a harder lead in a pencil.

It is possible to determine the amount of pressure by feeling the original sample with thumb and index finger, but since the writing could have been done on a hard surface, like glass, this is not accurate at all times. It is difficult also to determine force of pressure from photocopies and/or use of felt pens.

A quick glance at the writing sample can often reveal energy dispersion and the degree of retention and absorption of emotional experiences.

The writer who exerts heavy pressure is one who absorbs strong emotional impact from life experiences and who will remember these experiences for a long period of time. On the other hand, the light writer is impressionable but more quickly forgets the feelings of an experience in time. Light pressure writers recognize a situation readily; heavy-pressured writers can endure a stressful situation longer than the light-pressured writer.

Heavy Pressure Writer: Hard working, enthusiastic, go-getter, vitality, drive. Like to be kept active and stimulated by anything they do. Tend to have low tolerance for routine or long periods of inactivity.

As employers:
- Will expect employees to be equally hardworking and dedicated.
- Will have long working hours and will be irritated when others an unwilling to follow their example.
- Will approach all challenges with energy, determination, and single-mindedness.
- Always ready to tackle as many fresh projects as possible. More likely to use forceful persuasion than quiet diplomacy. Intolerant of employees who appear to be unoccupied or idle.
- Will favor high activity employees; will tolerate medium activity employees. (With this boss there is a need to look busy and overwhelmed with work at all times!)
- Low activity employees will be exhausted by the ceaseless demands, activity, and constant enthusiasm.

As employees:
- Will work best in jobs with plenty of stimulation and challenge.
- Will like working with public: selling, journalism.
- Will become restless for change if doing routine chores with too much detail and brain work.

Light Pressure Writer: Tends to have low energy, avoids strenuous activities for long periods, can lack enthusiasm and drive, even for things that really interest them. Usually prefer the familiar and routine to the unusual and changing.

As employers:
- Tend to show less interest in how employees are doing their job.
- Do not exert much authority or pressure on employees.
- Seldom willing to drive themselves or others.
- May over-delegate, shift responsibility, blame others if something goes wrong.
- Prefer secure routine and familiar work.
- Will leave employees alone to work at their own pace, free from constant pressure. Employee will not have to worry about change in routine, but may expect unfair criticism when things go wrong.
- Medium to high activity persons will be uncomfortable with this employer as expenditure of energy will be discouraged.

As employee:
- Unable to work under pressure for long periods or to cope with emergencies.
- Work best in routine work with methodical approach where they can use their eye for detail. Enthusiasm and initiative comes in spurts.
- Will work well in complaint department if procedure for handling complaints is spelled out.

They can be cool and objective about critical comments and abuse.

Medium Pressure Writers: Will maintain a balance between too much activity and too great a degree of sensitiveness to pressure. May lack the intense drive and enthusiasm of heavy writers, but will be better suited to work methodically at routine tasks. Tends to be more tolerant of inactivity of others.

As employer:
- Easiest and most pleasant for whom to work.
- Lacks the intense drive of the heavy writer boss, but still will expect a reasonable output of performance.
- Working for them will never be boring.
- Can work under pressure when needed, but see no point in treating every activity as an emergency.
- Other medium and light writers relate well to them; the heavy writers may be irritated at not being able to throw all of their energies into every single task.

As employees:
- Keep them busy to avoid loss of motivation and interest.
- Do not expect strenuous/highly demanding work for long periods of time.
- Will work 8 hours, go home, and forget the job until tomorrow.
- Will work best with a certain amount of routine interspersed with the stimulation of occasional challenge or unexpected change.
- Enjoys a fairly settle routine if it is broken up with occasional changes to make life more interesting.
- Will do everyday chores, but will put off the bigger

tasks. Happiest working with others of similar activity level. Find highly active work to energetic and low level too undemanding.

Cholerics and Melancholics usually write with heavy pressure. Sanguines and Phlegmatics usually write with lighter pressure.

4. **DUCTUS**: Pen chosen to channel the mental energy, physical energy and endurance.

Choleric–Thick/Sharp

looking forward to meeting information .

Sanguine–Thin/Sharp

needed gasoline before the train to New York. + the station on time

Melancholic–Thin/Pasty

There has been a long standing controversy as to whether photography is art. Painters

Phlegmatic–Thick/Pasty

I AWOKE THIS MORNING, I FOUND THE REFRIGERATOR TOTALLY EMPTY. I WAS PRETTY ANNOYED WITH BECAUSE I WAS STARVING. I WAS TOO LAZY

5. **Tempo**: Speed and movement flow. The way we write and the way we think bear a close relation.

— **Slow** *writing may indicate deliberateness, hesitation, inflexibility, and/or caution.*

— **Fast** writing may indicate strong feeling, quick thinking, energy, and/or need for change.

Caution: No personality exists in the absolute; so, an evaluation of the total personality is essential in identifying the combinations of writing which indicate personality types.

Cholerics usually write moderately fast;

Phlegmatics tend to write slow

Melancholics and Saguines write fast.

Slow

just opening or have only opened half-way. * Gather roses from your garden only in the morning or evening, when they're freshest; hot daytime sun robs them of moisture. * Revive wilted roses by submerging them entirely in tepid water for

Fast

Courtesy and friendliness. We have been trying to accomplish this goal since our grand opening. Training and attitude

The checklist that follows, compiled by Barbara Heinz Mc-Dermaid, will aid in determining the speed of the writing.

Graphic Indicators of Speed

Slow

___Controlled, monotonous, over-elaborate, clumsy, tremulous

___F- to BC slant remains about the same

___Very large or very small MZ

___Pasty writing, unvarying or displaced pressure

___Steady or decreasing left margin

___Steady or descending lines

___Letters significantly narrower or broader than tall

___Letter spacing significantly narrower or wider than MZ height

___Angle, angular arcade, double curve connectors

___Extensions less than 1 or greater than 3 times MZH

___Copybook or elaborated lead-ins

___Blunt or leftward-turning endings

___Round, circled, carefully placed i dots

___Short t-bars to left of stem or exactly placed

___ Total Slow

Graphic Indicators of Speed

Fast

___Released, animated, natural, spontaneous writing

___BC to E+ slant may increase as writing progresses

___Sizable MZ (3mm)

___Sharp writing; pressure alternates naturally

___Increasing left margin

___Ascending lines

___Letters approximately as wide as they are tall

___Letter spacing approximately the same as MZ height

___Garland, thread, sharks tooth, or mixed connectors

___Extensions from 1-3 times MZ height

___Short, simplified beginnings of letters; not lead-ins

___Feathered or hooked endings

___Jagged i dots, carelessly placed or connected to next letter

___Long t-bars to right of stem or connected to next letter

___ Total Fast

6. Form—Letter Configuration

Determined by contour, shape, ornamentation, curvature, progression of a stroke with speed and legibility.

Choleric-Mixed

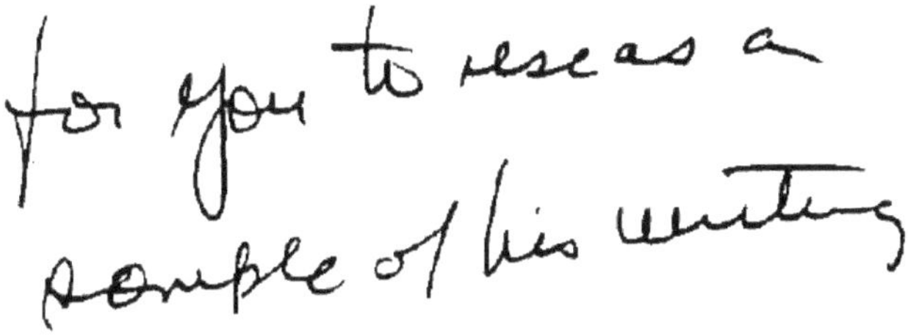
for you to see as a
sample of his writing

Sanguine-Oval

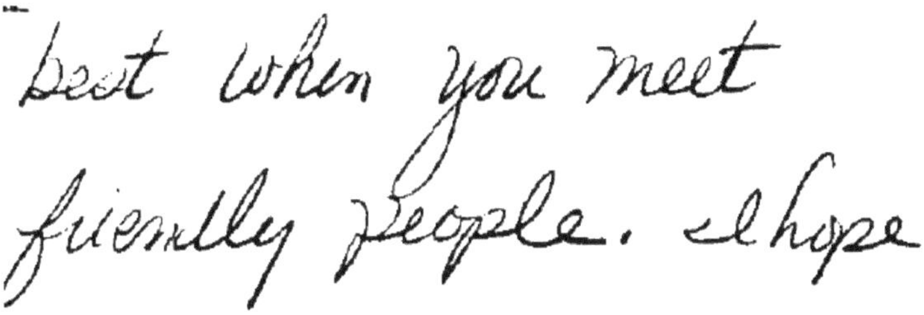
best when you meet
friendly people. I hope

Melancholic-Angular

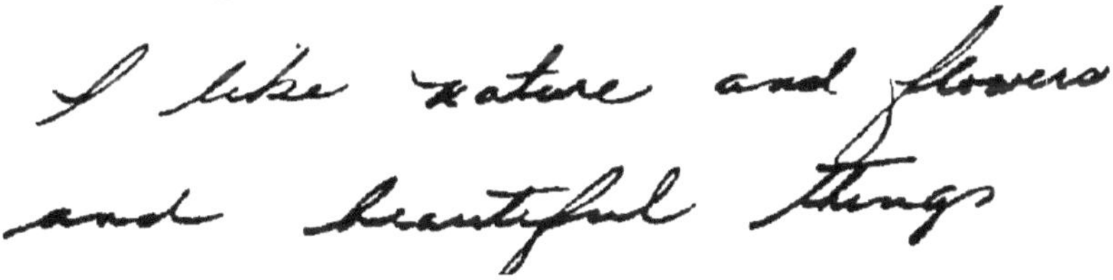
I like nature and flowers
and beautiful things

Phlegmatic-Round

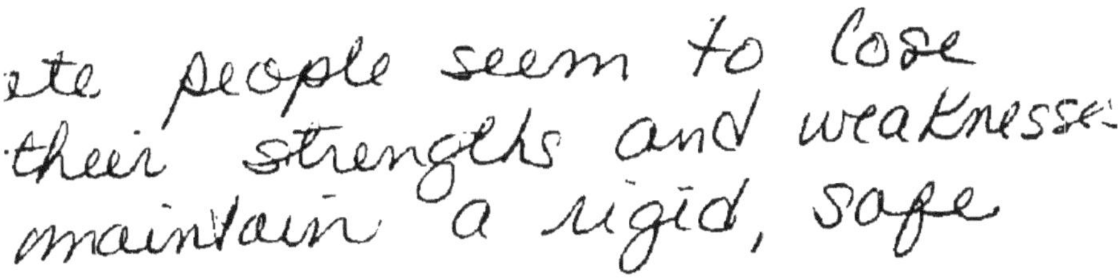
people seem to lose
their strengths and weaknesse
maintain a rigid, safe

7. Stability: characteristics of balance.

All zone developed and measurable to themselves, consistency of stroke formations and rhythm, harmonious movement, poise, and discipline.

Choleric-Moderate

I like snow flakes and Swimming. I like babies and people.

Sanguine-Variable

a wonderful dream. is wonderful and I

Melancholic-Regular

was sending this letter. The lady want . teaching position. Her past experience

Phlegmatic-Precise

My heart truely does overflow with thanks for the Smiles, sunshine, and happy

8. Letter Pattern (style)

Choleric-Simplified

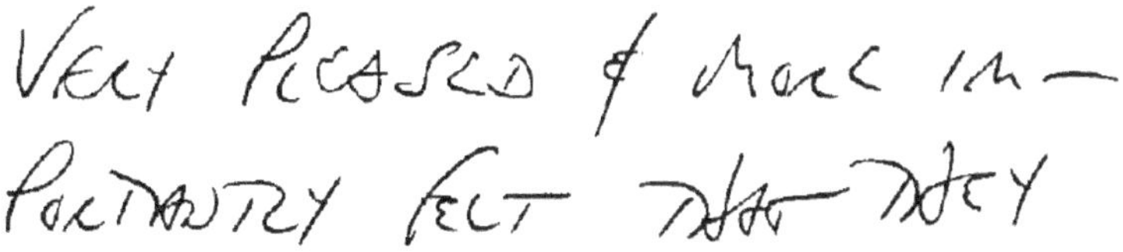
VERY PLEASED & MORE IM-
PORTANTLY FELT THAT THEY

Sanguine-Elaborated

Take care. We all love you very much.

Melancholic-Copybook

I like handwriting analysis.

Phlegmatic–Enlarged or very small

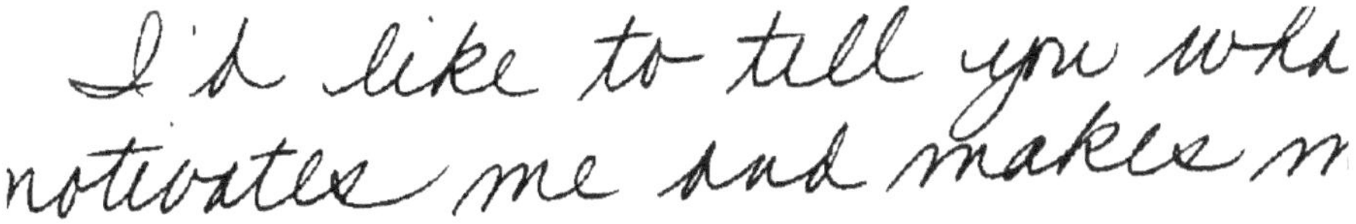
I'd like to tell you
motivates me and makes

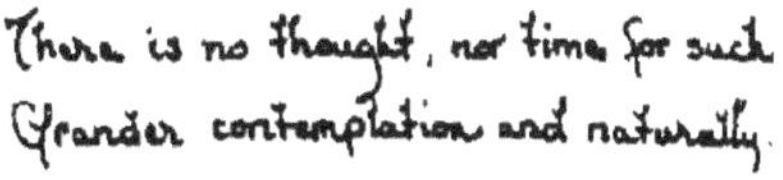
There is no thought, nor time for such
Grander contemplation and naturally.

9. Height: Middle zone vertical measurement

Choleric-Moderate *you a course*

Sanguine-Tall *many interesting*

Melancholic-Small *been attending classes*

Phlegmatic-Moderate *have* *the smile and*

(Very large or very small)

10. Width—Middle zone horizontal measurement

Choleric-Moderate *hot new sample,*

Sanguine-Wide *to travel*

Melancholic-Narrow *great interest*

Phlegmatic-Very Wide *love to*

11. Area Size (These are guides, not absolutes)

Choleric - 1 ½ (measure MZ. UZ 1x MX measurement. LZ 2x MZ)

LESSEN my ANXIETY

Sanguine - 2 ½ (measure MZ. UZ 2x MZ. LZ 2x MZ)

enough requirements,

Melancholic - 3/1/1 (Measure MZ. UZ 3x MZ. LZ 1x MZ)

people who have completed

Phlegmatic - ½ - 1 ½ (Measure MZ. UZ ½ x MZ. LZ ½ MZ)

Most people must

12. d/t Stem — If looped

Choleric- Short/Narrow   *pleased*   *and*

Sanguine-Tall/Narrow   *figured*   *Tuesday*

Melancholic-Tall/Wide   *amfindebted*   *cold*

Phlegmatic-Short/Narrow   *changed*   *hard*

CHECKLIST FOR GRAPHIC INDICATORS Of SPEED

WORKSHEET

FACTOR	CHOLERIC (Elephant)	SANGUINE (Butterfly)
Gestalt	dynamic, purposive, vital	restless, frivolous, expansive
Slant	BC-E+	BC-DE
Pressure	Heavy	Moderate
Ductus	Thick/sharp	Thin/sharp
*Tempo	Moderate	Fast
Form	Mixed	Oval
Stability	Moderate	Variable
Letter Pattern	Simplified	Elaborated
*Height	Moderate	Tall
*Width	Moderate	Wide
*Area Size	1/1/2	2/1/2
d/t stem-if looped	Short/narrow	Tall/narrow

Factor	Melancholic (Frog)	Phlegmatic (Turtle)
Gestalt	intense, agitated, repressed	relaxed, soft, calm
Slant	CD-E+	FA-BC
*Pressure	Very heavy	Light
Ductus	Thin/pasty	Thick/pasty
*Tempo	Fairly fast	Slow
Form	Angular	Round
Stability	Regular	Precise
Letter Pattern	Copybook	Enlarged
*Height	Small	Moderate
*Width	Narrow	Very wide
*Area Size	3/1/1	1/2-1-1/2
d/t stem-if looped	Tall/wide	Short/narrow

_____ *Most important factors for rapid check   (Fr. N. Werling)

Enjoying Your Work And Your Leisure

Many gifted people go through life getting little satisfaction and less joy in the nine to five workplace; then they go home to an even more drab existence. This is not necessary and can be changed through serious introspection, a study of temperament and the life styles, work styles, and leisure styles that can be most productive to each temperament. It is vitally important for each of us to discover the niche in life in which we will be most successful, productive, and happy. The following suggestions of possible vocations and avocations are given as a help to making this all-important discovery.

CHOLERICS: These elephants will do well in any job that calls for working with people in a leadership, management, organizational, construction, or supervisory role—in fact, they will feel most fulfilled whenever they are facing new frontiers and overcoming apparently insurmountable obstacles. They are not happy with jobs that require too much detail, but can usually delegate this to a frog or turtle in their employ. Finding new ways to surmount difficulties in a difficult Job goes with the powerful, strong, restless, competitive drive that leads them on to super-stardom.

We find them happily functioning in the workplace as Administrators—(construction superintendents, foremen, supervisors, farm managers, operators of heavy equipment, head carpenter, cement workers, landscapers, clerks of the works); Entrepreneurs— (any new business venture that includes profit risk); Executives in all fields; Lawyers—(attorneys, district attorneys, tax attorneys, judges, patent agents); Investigators—(building inspectors, postal inspectors, patrolmen, park ranger, claims adjusters); Leaders—chairpersons of the board, presidents of organizations, captains of the team, owners of the business); Organizers; Politicians—local, state, national; Producers—radio, TV, Movie; Health services—chef, surgeons, dentists, general practitioners, cardiologists, head nurses, physical and occupational therapists; Law enforcement officers—(police chiefs, sheriffs, parole and probation officers); and Transportation.

Avocations/hobbies: Elephants will choose outdoor activities for their relaxation: golf, sports, mountain climbing, sailing—in fact anything that requires physical endurance and an opportunity to compete either with others or with their own record.
Well-known Cholerics: Ronald Reagan, Winston Churchill, Lee Iacocca, Vince Lombardi, Margaret Thatcher

SANGUINES: These warm, happy, outgoing butterflies work best with and for others. Since they enjoy activity, recognition, attention, and change, they are at their best in jobs that encourage these qualities. They are best suited for the Arts and Humanities: fine arts, art work and decorating, photography, dramatics, radio and TV, dance, specialty entertainment work, physical entertainment work, recreation work, and sales.

At their best in vocations that call for empathy and human service, they make excellent receptionists, secretaries, masters of ceremony, fund raisers, flight attendants, cruise directors, teachers, visiting and caring for the sick and helpless—in fact, any work that calls for personal service which gives them opportunity to express their inborn empathy while helping to make people happy.

Avocations and hobbies: Cooking, entertaining, participation in athletics, shopping— (window and otherwise), partying, group activities which give them the opportunity to get away from the humdrum, usual and boring work at hand. They are fun to be with and always seem to be having the time of their lives.

Well-known Sanguines: Dolly Parton, Ginger Rogers, Robert Redford, Helen Hayes, Olivia Newton John, James Cagney

MELANCHOLICS: These quiet, introverted frogs are content in any vocation that calls forth their innate need for creativity, analytical ability, emotional response, self -sacrifice, and perfection. Intelligence and analytical ability help them to become outstanding engineers and inventors, while their deep desire to help others makes them outstanding educators, (particularly as college professors), ministers, preachers, reformers, caregivers, humanitarians, nurses, doctors, and performing artists in music, art, and on the stage. (They make excellent actors/actresses and surprising others by abandoning their strong introvert tendencies when on stage.)

Avocations and hobbies: spectator sports, writing poetry, cooking, sewing, crafts, and anything that calls forth their highly creative gifts and quiet enjoyment of aesthetic activities.

Well-known Melancholics: Martin Luther King, Jimmy Carter, Billy Graham

PHLEGMATICS: these relaxed, solitary, peaceful, calm turtles, do well in any environment that calls for neat, proficient, thorough, organized, slow-moving activities. They are noted for their ability to negotiate, bring order out of disorder, and effect a stabilizing influence on the work force.

We find them at their best in education, engineering, and personnel work. Specifically,   they make gracious librarians; counselors   with remarkable skill for listening; prudent and calm diplomats; researchers; technicians, statisticians, and scientists; devoted teachers—particularly, working with small children or students who find learning difficult, as well as in colleges and universities; psychologists; mechanics; researchers; cooks; therapists; accountants; computer analysts; nurses; mechanics; chemical and civil engineers.

They work well under pressure, having a stabilizing effect on others who work with them, bringing humor, calm and routine to their everyday lives.

Avocations and hobbies: gourmet cook, cartoonist, stand-up comedian, chess player, sports watcher, people watcher, bird watcher, crafts, reading (particularly mystery stories), fishing, and thinking, (Turtles are the thinkers of the world.) Good company they keep with other turtles: Edison, Marx, Plato, Aristotle, Einstein, Thomas Aquinas.

"I can do it myself."   "Let's try it!"   "It won't work."   "Today?"

The Elephant Crashes onto the Page

I ENJOY THE WEATHER
BECAUSE IT IS NOT HUMID.

meeting, having had 2 cups of strong

nice to hear from you - that you

now that the analysis is over
feel free to write to you!? I

have changes or questions. WE have

If you are really going

with those specific questions. I plan on

on my mind, I would like

54

The Butterfly Flutters Onto the Page

It is only with the heart that one
can see rightly what is essential

I have a hobby in the house
that I enjoy and several pursuits

Now I am writing another
expression of myself, considering
perhaps the fearful possibility that
I have not thoroughly represented

I am sending you a sample of handwriting
of a man in my life, do you see any
negative traits in his writing that I would

and ~~talking~~ thank you
for all your support

terms and believe in your ability to
accurately describe a personaly any

The Frog Leaps Onto the Page

Most people must learn more to earn more. The most important learning is an understanding of human nature. This naturally should start with a study of

tripple your anual income. Many people who have completed our special

him, nor to understand and meet his

of human nature This naturally should start with a study of self. Please prepare

strongly from all my experiences that his Mom would not be able to handle

good friends with. She and I used to date quite often and even go out of as friends real often with she never took to Dan Jose since then she, has

56

The Turtle Crawls Onto the Page

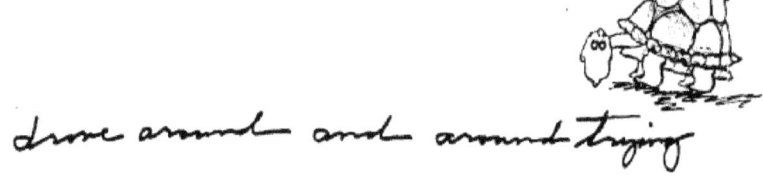

drove around and around trying

one I received for Christmas
and in reading it have

There is even a deeper objection. I don't know exactly
what I shall say in these lectures. When one accepts
a lectureship because one has, at that moment never

I enjoy foreign language study because the
exploration opens new and different avenues of
communication with other cultures and people,
broadens the intellect and presents a considerable

For instance just for class we had

The main reason that I would like to
have my handwriting analyzed is because
have come to a point in my life where

is he just an over enthusiastic
storyteller? I'd hate to misjudge

CHAPTER THREE

Identifying The Primary And Secondary Temperaments

Analysts who work with temperament soon realize that, although all four temperaments are represented in a given personality, two (and at rare times three) temperaments are represented in a strong combination. The first temperament is always seen in the handwriting, the second is often discovered through the body structure. Most people have a mixed blend of temperaments, with traits from one or more other temperaments, one of which will be predominant.

The dark and light sides of the predominant temperament are highlighted or extended by the influence of the qualities of the secondary temperament. This combination softens the harsh characteristics of the main temperament and leads to a happy blend. Occasionally, the bright side of the secondary temperament cancels out the harsh qualities of the main temperament. Possibilities of blends are numerous, accounting for the surprising differences in behavior, endeavor, motivation, ability, skill, accomplishment, and personality styles that make some individuals seem so complex.

For the sake of simplicity, we will describe only twelve of these blends, but it is well to remember that traits from other temperaments may show up and the degrees of intensity can differ in the temperament blends, changing the

actions and reactions of one choleric/ sanguine temperament from that of another who might also be classified as
choleric/ sanguine.

The **Choleric/ Sanguine** (CS) temperament is identified by a quick excitement and reaction to experiences, although the impression is not so lasting as with the pure
choleric temperament. The pride of the choleric is mixed
with the vanity of the sanguine and the anger and obsti-
nacy are more moderate than in the pure choleric. This
makes for a happier combination. Both of these temperaments are outer-directed which makes the elephant/but-
terfly blend a strong, highly motivated, success-oriented,
and very active-oriented person.

The **Sanguine/Choleric** (SC) temperament is similar
to the choleric/ sanguine temperament, but since the sanguine characteristics are combined with the choleric, impressions do not fade as rapidly as with the pure sanguine.
At the same time, there is a light-heartedness and love of
variety that is not evident in the elephant/butterfly combination.

Changeableness, superficiality, and talkativeness are
toned down by the seriousness and stability of the choleric. This butterfly/elephant, a complete extrovert type, is
a fun person always on the go and always ready for excitement. The traits of the choleric help to give organization
and more stability to the temperament them is found in the
pure sanguine.

The **Choleric/Melancholic** (CM) and the **Melan-
cholic/Choleric** (MC) present a mixture of two serious,
passionate temperaments. The enthusiasm, determination, independence, optimism, and extroversion of the choleric combine well with the analytical, easily discouraged,
realistically pessimistic, introverted, melancholic traits.

The pride, stubbornness, and anger of the choleric are tempered by the fretful, gloomy, unsocial, reserved, inner-directed attitude of the melancholic. Both mixtures present highly capable, gifted, idealistic persons. However, the frog/elephants, possibly the most gifted of all the blends, find it difficult to achieve their potential because of moodiness, a natural suspicion of others, and sensitiveness to any criticism.

In the **Melancholic/Sanguine** (MS) temperament impressions are not strong, reactions are weak and do not last as long as in the pure melancholic. The sanguine traits add flexibility, friendliness, and cheerfulness to the melancholic. Frogs with a butterfly secondary temperament are those highly gifted, cordial, soft-hearted people who cannot bear to hurt anyone or see anyone treated unjustly. They are emotionally responsive, moody, and often inclined to negative thinking. They fail where energy and strength are needed. This temperament, while not so introverted as the pure melancholic, needs to develop the extroverted qualities of the sanguine to become friendly and sociable.

The opposite combination of the **Sanguine/Melancholic** (SM) is the most emotional of the temperament blends. These butterfly/ frogs are capable of swinging from a high mood to a low one almost instantaneously. Because of the outgoing assets of the sanguine, this temperament is more outgoing and sociable than the frog/butterfly. Since both sanguines and melancholics are inclined to dream rather than to act, there is a need for motivation and goal-set ting to assure that butterfly/frogs reach the latent potential of their highly gifted, dramatic selves.

The **Choleric/Phlegmatic** CCM) temperament combination presents an interesting blend of fiery enthusiasm with a slow, easygoing, and practical efficiency. The pragmatic, hard-working, attention to detail of the phlegmatic, tempers the quick, impulsive, aggressiveness of the choleric, who is able to organize and plan, but dislikes the monotony of detailed work which is necessary for success.

The quiet good humor of the phlegmatic tones down the irascibility of the quick-moving choleric. Both the choleric and the phlegmatic are stubborn, but the low energy of the phlegmatic often disguises this determination, and the refusal to go along will be so quiet and unobtrusive that it will scarcely be evident to the casual observer. This elephant/ turtle blend has great possibilities.

The most uninhibited temperament blend is without doubt the **Sanguine/Phlegmatic** (SM) type. These happy-go-lucky, lovable, good-humored people spend their lives trying to find ways to help others stay happy. The qualities of the outgoing, noisy, mercurial, pleasure-seeking sanguine are toned down by the friendly, easy-going, dependable, faithful phlegmatic. Likewise, the energy and enthusiasm of the sanguine help to motivate the slow-moving, quiet, efficient phlegmatic.

A danger with this butterfly/turtle combination comes from the sanguines lack of perseverance, combined with the phlegmatics lack of energy. Without motivation and a loving environment, persons of this temperament could easily settle back and accomplish very little.

Individuals with the **Melancholic/Phlegmatic** (MP) blend succeed better in social situations than the pure melancholic. Lacking, more or less, the ill-tempered, gloomy, brooding tendencies of the melancholics, they are happily aided by the quiet apathy of the phlegmatic. These gifted introverts are not easily of fended, can bear injuries patiently, and are contented, steady workers. They combine the analytical thinking, the rich, sensitive, emotionally responsive traits of the melancholic with the cheerful, good-natured, organized practicality of the phlegmatic.

This complementary combination usually spells great success.

Frog/turtles get along well with others, are natural peacemakers and humanitarians. Although the frog/ turtle type presents a double introvert, the steadiness and humor of the phlegmatic help to bring out the gift of the melancholic, while the deep reflective thinking and self-centered trait s of the melancholic, which often lead to suspicion '3nd hurt feeling, are tempered by the dry sense of humor and natural amiability of the phlegmatic.

The combination of **Phlegmatic/Choleric** (PC) presents the most highly motivated of the phlegmatic types, yet the weaknesses, particularly indecision, fear, and lack of enthusiasm, of ten keep PC's from attaining great success in life.

These people are more often found working for others, supplying the detail, organization, and efficiency so necessary for success. The lack of drive which often characterizes the phlegmatic is overcome by the goal-oriented tendencies of the choleric, while the diplomacy and tactful response to others of the phlegmatic temper the outspoken, abrasive manner of the choleric.

The tendencies of indecision, fear, and a thin-skinned approach to life of the phlegmatic will be softened by the decisiveness, courage, and objectiveness of the choleric. The outgoing, talkative, enthusiastic, and generous qualities of the choleric help to overcome the lack of involvement, quiet, unmotivated, stingy weaknesses of the phlegmatic. With training and motivation this turtle/elephant temperament blend has a great deal to offer.

The **Phlegmatic/Sanguine** (PS) type is the gentlest, most lovable, and least obtrusive of all the temperament types. This combination of the outer-directed, warm, buoyant, naturally receptive butterfly with the inner-directed, easy-going, calm, composed, peace-loving, well-balanced, thoughtful, practical, loyal, humorous turtle presents what on the surface appears to be the perfect personality.

However, without considerable prodding from those about them, particularly when they are young, persons of this temperament blend could become a great disappointment to others and to themselves. The weaknesses of both types are so similar that they can lead to a life of inertia. A particular problem is that both temperaments are so gentle, w arm, and friendly that their weaknesses are not easily apparent until they have become too entrenched for improvement. Since neither the phlegmatic nor the sanguine is highly motivated or self-disciplined, without help from others, they easily lapse into laziness and indecision.

The Double Introvert

Finally, we come to another double introvert, the **Phlegmatic/Melancholic** (PM) The PM is the most quiet, gentle, and passive of all the temperament blends. Everything done by the turtle/ frog is slow, deliberate, detailed, organized, and without flaw—possibly not finished, unless ample time is set aside for completion—but what is done is flawless.

These quiet turtle/ frogs spend many hours quietly thinking about the task at hand, mapping it out so that it will be perfect when completed—if completed. They work happily and contentedly, speaking little, working, for the most part, in happy isolation or with other quiet turtle/ frogs. Noise and confusion are repulsive to them. They prefer to do their work without interference from others, spending many hours organizing and planning what they wish to accomplish. On the weakness side, they tend to procrastinate, mistrusting themselves (in spite of their great talent), fearing failure, preferring to be spectators rather than innovators, worrying about the possibility that they might be called upon to overextend themselves. Because of their calm, quiet, patient, efficient, humorous, and kind nature, they make excellent counselors and teachers.

With careful study it should be possible for each of us to determine what primary and secondary temperaments control our activities. It is particularly important that we try to understand the temperaments of those with whom we live or work in order to make allowances for their particular peculiarities, strengths, weaknesses, and talents. If we educate children, our own or others, it is of prime importance for us to know that motivates or turns off the child. A program of educating children or adults to understand themselves will go far toward creating a better world in which to pay and work.

Main Characteristics and Possible Blends

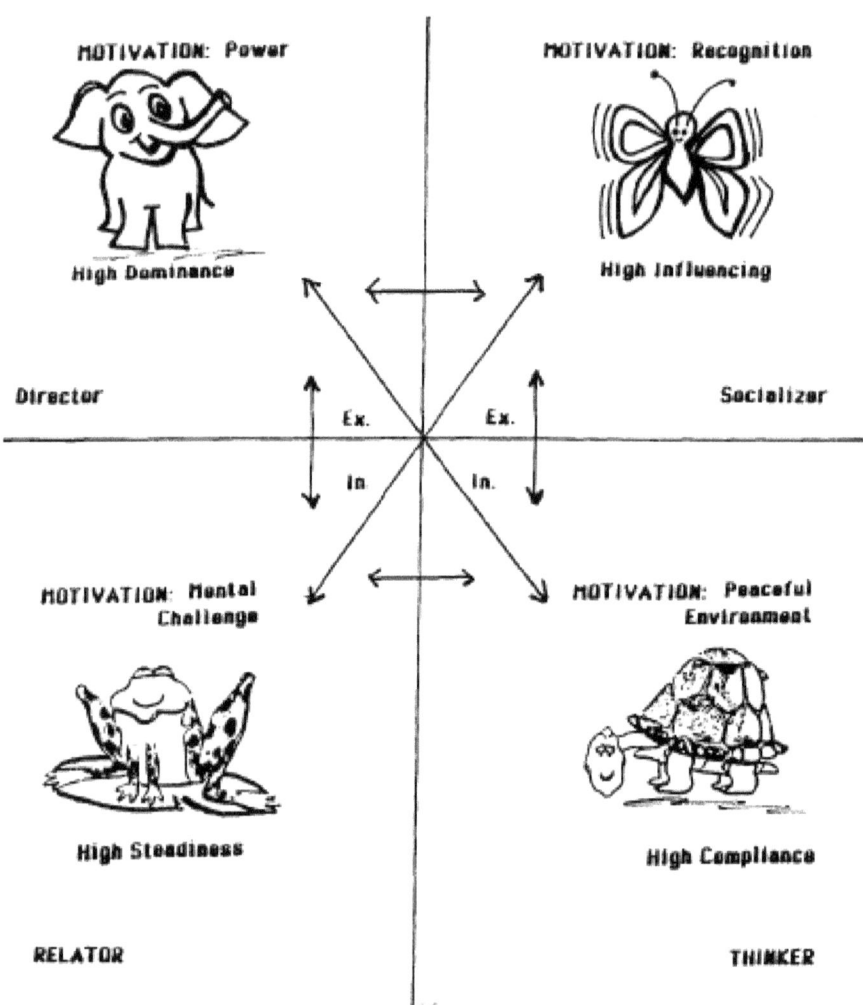

TEMPERAMENT WORKSHEET

FACTOR	Choleric Elephant	Sanguine Butterfly	Melancholic Frog	Phlegmatic Turtle
Gestalt	**X** dynamic vital	restless frivolous	intense repressed	relaxed calm
Slant	BC -E+	BC - DE	**X** CD-E+	FA-BC
*Pressure	Heavy	**X** Moderate	Very heavy	Light
Ductus	Thick/sharp	**X** Thin/sharp	Thin/pasty	Thick/pasty
*Tempo	Moderate	**X** Fast	Fairly fast	Slow
Form	**X** Mixed	Oval	Angular	Round
Stability	**X** Moderate	Variable	Regular	Precise
Ltr pattern	**X** Simplified	Elaborated	Copybook	Enlarged
*Height	**X** Moderate	Tall	Small	Moderate
*Width	Moderate	Wide	**X** Narrow	Very wide
*Area Size	**X** 1/1/2	2/1/2	3/1/1	1/2-1-1/2
D/t stem If looped	Short/ narrow	Tall/ narrow	Tall/ wide	Short/ narrow
Total:	6 ____	3 ____	2 ____	____

*Most important factors for rapid check
Temperament: Choleric/Sanguine

My handwriting looks different to
me sometimes, so I tried to "speed up"
and give you an example of the

TEMPERAMENT WORKSHEET

FACTOR	Choleric Elephant	Sanguine Butterfly	Melancholic Frog	Phlegmatic Turtle
Gestalt **X**	Dynamic Vital	Restless Expansive	Intense Agitated	Relaxed Calm
Slant **X**	BC -E+	BC - DE	CD-E+	FA-BC
*Pressure **X**	Heavy	Moderate	Very heavy	Light
Ductus	Thick/sharp	Thin/sharp **X**	Thin/pasty	Thick/pasty
*Tempo	Moderate	Fast **X**	Fairly fast	Slow
Form **X**	Mixed	Oval	Angular	Round
Stability **X**	Moderate	Variable	Regular	Precise
Ltr pattern **X**	Simplified	Elaborated	Copybook	Enlarged
*Height **X**	Moderate	Tall	Small	Moderate
*Width **X**	Moderate	Wide	Narrow	Very wide
*Area Size	1/1/2 **X**	2/1/2	3/1/1	1/2-1-1/2
D/t stem If looped	Short/ narrow **X**	Tall/ narrow	Tall/ wide	Short/ narrow
Total:	7	2	3	

*Most important factors for rapid check
Temperament: Choleric/Melancholic

for any interest in joining in a such executive position i.s, that the highest regard for the parent company

144

TEMPERAMENT WORKSHEET

FACTOR	Choleric Elephant	Sanguine Butterfly	Melancholic Frog	Phlegmatic Turtle
Gestalt **X**	Dynamic Vital	Restless Expansive	Intense Agitated	Relaxed Calm
Slant	BC -E+	BC - DE	CD-E+ **X**	FA-BC
*Pressure **X**	Heavy	Moderate	Very heavy	Light
Ductus	Thick/sharp	Thin/sharp	Thin/pasty **X**	Thick/pasty
*Tempo **X**	Moderate	Fast	Fairly fast	Slow
Form **X**	Mixed	Oval	Angular	Round
Stability	Moderate **X**	Variable	Regular	Precise
Ltr pattern **X**	Simplified	Elaborated	Copybook	Enlarged
*Height **X**	Moderate	Tall	Small **X**	Moderate
*Width **X**	Moderate	Wide	Narrow	Very wide
*Area Size	1/1/2 **X**	2/1/2	3/1/1	1/2-1-1/2
D/t stem If looped	Short/ narrow **X**	Tall/ narrow	Tall/ wide	Short/ narrow
Total:	8	1		4

*Most important factors for rapid check
Temperament: Choleric/Phlegmatic

I plan to enroll in your
hand writing class in Sept. I'm
especially interested in learning
about which traits are more

TEMPERAMENT WORKSHEET

FACTOR	Choleric Elephant	Sanguine Butterfly	Melancholic Frog	Phlegmatic Turtle
Gestalt	Dynamic Vital	Restless Expansive	Intense Agitated	**X** Relaxed Calm
Slant	BC -E+	**X** BC - DE	CD-E+	FA-BC
*Pressure	Heavy	**X** Moderate	Very heavy	Light
Ductus	**X** Thick/sharp	Thin/sharp	**X** Thin/pasty	Thick/pasty
*Tempo	Moderate	**X** Fast	Fairly fast	Slow
Form	**X** Mixed	Oval	Angular	Round
Stability	Moderate	**X** Variable	Regular	Precise
Ltr pattern	**X** Simplified	Elaborated	Copybook	Enlarged
*Height	Moderate	**X** Tall	Small	Moderate
*Width	Moderate	**X** Wide	Narrow	Very wide
*Area Size	1/1/2	**X** 2/1/2	3/1/1	1/2-1-1/2
D/t stem If looped	**X** Short/ narrow	Tall/ narrow	Tall/ wide	Short/ narrow
Total:	4	7		1

*Most important factors for rapid check

Temperament: Sanguine/Choleric

[handwritten:] times it seems they were too beautiful to be anything bu a dream. How did um

146

TEMPERAMENT WORKSHEET

FACTOR	Choleric Elephant	Sanguine Butterfly	Melancholic Frog	Phlegmatic Turtle
Gestalt	Dynamic Vital **X**	Restless Expansive	Intense Agitated	Relaxed Calm
Slant	BC -E+	BC - DE **X**	CD-E+	FA-BC
*Pressure	Heavy **X**	Moderate	Very heavy	Light
Ductus	Thick/sharp **X**	Thin/sharp	Thin/pasty	Thick/pasty
*Tempo	Moderate **X**	Fast	Fairly fast	Slow
Form	Mixed	Oval **X**	Angular	Round
Stability	Moderate **X**	Variable	Regular	Precise
Ltr pattern	Simplified **X**	Elaborated	Copybook	Enlarged
*Height	Moderate **X**	Tall	Small	Moderate
*Width	Moderate	Wide **X**	Narrow	Very wide
*Area Size	1/1/2 **X**	2/1/2	3/1/1	1/2-1-1/2
D/t stem If looped	Short/ narrow	Tall/ narrow	Tall/ wide	Short/ narrow
Total:		8	3	

*Most important factors for rapid check
Temperament: Sanguine/Melancholic

I'm really "On the Road Again" 😊 with a very busy schedule —but everything is going beautifully.

TEMPERAMENT WORKSHEET

FACTOR	Choleric Elephant	Sanguine Butterfly	Melancholic Frog	Phlegmatic Turtle
Gestalt **X**	Dynamic Vital	Restless Expansive	Intense Agitated	Relaxed Calm
Slant **X**	BC -E+	BC - DE	CD-E+	FA-BC
*Pressure **X**	Heavy	Moderate	Very heavy	Light
Ductus	Thick/sharp	Thin/sharp **X**	Thin/pasty	Thick/pasty
*Tempo	Moderate	Fast	Fairly fast	Slow
Form	Mixed	Oval	Angular	Round
Stability	Moderate	Variable	Regular	Precise
Ltr pattern	Simplified	Elaborated	Copybook	Enlarged
*Height	Moderate	Tall	Small	Moderate
*Width	Moderate	Wide	Narrow	Very wide
*Area Size	1/1/2	2/1/2	3/1/1	1/2-1-1/2
D/t stem If looped	Short/ narrow	Tall/ narrow	Tall/ wide	Short/ narrow
Total:	____	____	____	____

*Most important factors for rapid check
Temperament: Sanguine/Phlegmatic

The hours spent will create a weekend event that will move us upward toward the

148

TEMPERAMENT WORKSHEET

FACTOR	Choleric Elephant	Sanguine Butterfly	Melancholic Frog	Phlegmatic Turtle
Gestalt	Dynamic Vital	Restless X Expansive	Intense Agitated	Relaxed Calm
Slant X	BC -E+	BC - DE	CD-E+	FA-BC
*Pressure	Heavy	Moderate X	Very heavy	Light
Ductus	Thick/sharp	Thin/sharp X	Thin/pasty	Thick/pasty
*Tempo	Moderate	Fast	X Fairly fast	Slow
Form X	Mixed	Oval	Angular	Round
Stability X	Moderate	Variable	Regular	Precise
Ltr pattern X	Simplified	Elaborated	Copybook	Enlarged
*Height	Moderate	Tall X	Small	Moderate
*Width	Moderate	Wide X	Narrow	Very wide
*Area Size	1/1/2	2/1/2 X	3/1/1	1/2-1-1/2
D/t stem If looped	Short/ narrow	Tall/ narrow X	Tall/ wide	Short/ narrow
Total:	4		8	

*Most important factors for rapid check
Temperament: Melancholic/Choleric

*been sunk in about 100' of water
off Ft. Lauderdale. The ship had
been down for only a few month
so there was not a great deal*

TEMPERAMENT WORKSHEET

FACTOR	Choleric Elephant	Sanguine Butterfly	Melancholic Frog	Phlegmatic Turtle
Gestalt	Dynamic Vital	Restless Expansive	Intense **X** Agitated	Relaxed Calm
Slant **X**	BC -E+	BC - DE	CD-E+	FA-BC
*Pressure	Heavy	Moderate	Very heavy **X**	Light
Ductus	Thick/sharp	Thin/sharp **X**	Thin/pasty	Thick/pasty
*Tempo	Moderate	Fast **X**	Fairly fast	Slow
Form	Mixed **X**	Oval	Angular	Round
Stability	Moderate **X**	Variable	Regular	Precise
Ltr pattern	Simplified **X**	Elaborated	Copybook	Enlarged
*Height	Moderate **X**	Tall	Small	Moderate
*Width	Moderate	Wide **X**	Narrow	Very wide
*Area Size	1/1/2	2/1/2 **X**	3/1/1	1/2-1-1/2
D/t stem If looped	Short/ narrow	Tall/ narrow **X**	Tall/ wide	Short/ narrow
Total:	1	4	5	2
	___	___	___	___

*Most important factors for rapid check
Temperament: Melancholic/Sanguine

As long as I have time to enjoy my family and friends, I'm happy.

150

TEMPERAMENT WORKSHEET

FACTOR	Choleric Elephant	Sanguine Butterfly	Melancholic Frog	Phlegmatic Turtle
Gestalt	Dynamic Vital	Restless Expansive	X Intense Agitated	Relaxed Calm
Slant	BC -E+ X	BC - DE	CD-E+	FA-BC
*Pressure	Heavy	Moderate	Very heavy X	Light
Ductus	Thick/sharp	Thin/sharp	X Thin/pasty	Thick/pasty
*Tempo	Moderate	Fast	Fairly fast X	Slow
Form	Mixed	Oval X	Angular	Round
Stability	Moderate	Variable	Regular X	Precise
Ltr pattern	Simplified	Elaborated X	Copybook	Enlarged
*Height	Moderate	Tall	Small X	Moderate
*Width	Moderate	Wide X	Narrow	Very wide
*Area Size	1/1/2 X	2/1/2	3/1/1	1/2-1-1/2
D/t stem If looped	Short/ narrow	Tall/ narrow	Tall/ wide	Short/ narrow
Total:		2	5	4

*Most important factors for rapid check
Temperament: Melancholic/Phlegmatic

Most people want learn more, to earn more. The most important learning is an understanding of human nature. This naturally should start with a study of self. Please prepare for me a brief check list of personality traits.

TEMPERAMENT WORKSHEET

FACTOR	Choleric Elephant	Sanguine Butterfly	Melancholic Frog	Phlegmatic Turtle
Gestalt X	Dynamic Vital	Restless Expansive	Intense Agitated	Relaxed Calm
Slant	BC -E+	BC - DE	CD-E+ X	FA-BC
*Pressure X	Heavy	Moderate	Very heavy	Light
Ductus	Thick/sharp	Thin/sharp	Thin/pasty X	Thick/pasty
*Tempo X	Moderate	Fast	Fairly fast	Slow
Form	Mixed	Oval	Angular X	Round
Stability	Moderate	Variable	Regular X	Precise
Ltr pattern	Simplified	Elaborated	Copybook X	Enlarged
*Height	Moderate	Tall	Small X	Moderate
*Width	Moderate	Wide	Narrow X	Very wide
*Area Size	1/1/2 X	2/1/2	3/1/1	1/2-1-1/2
D/t stem X If looped	Short/ narrow	Tall/ narrow	Tall/ wide	Short/ narrow
Total:	4	1		7
	———	———	———	———

*Most important factors for rapid check
Temperament: Phlegmatic/Choleric

or left to accommodate one or more formulas of up to 80 steps. So that

TEMPERAMENT WORKSHEET

FACTOR	Choleric Elephant	Sanguine Butterfly	Melancholic Frog	Phlegmatic Turtle
Gestalt	Dynamic Vital	Restless Expansive	Intense X Agitated	Relaxed Calm
Slant	BC -E+	BC - DE	CD-E+ X	FA-BC
*Pressure	Heavy X	Moderate	Very heavy	Light
Ductus X	Thick/sharp	Thin/sharp	Thin/pasty	Thick/pasty
*Tempo	Moderate	Fast	Fairly fast X	Slow
Form	Mixed	Oval	Angular X	Round
Stability	Moderate X	Variable	Regular	Precise
Ltr pattern	Simplified	Elaborated	Copybook X	Enlarged
*Height	Moderate	Tall	Small X	Moderate
*Width	Moderate X	Wide	Narrow	Very wide
*Area Size X	1/1/2	2/1/2	3/1/1	1/2-1-1/2
D/t stem If looped	Short/ narrow	Tall/ narrow	Tall/ wide	Short/ narrow
Total:	2	3		6

*Most important factors for rapid check

Temperament: Phlegmatic/Sanguine

is settling down with a new preferably one that is thick It doesn't have to be uacy,

153

TEMPERAMENT WORKSHEET

FACTOR	Choleric Elephant	Sanguine Butterfly	Melancholic Frog	Phlegmatic Turtle
Gestalt	Dynamic Vital	Restless Expansive	Intense **X** Agitated	Relaxed Calm
Slant	BC -E+	BC - DE **X**	CD-E+	FA-BC
*Pressure	Heavy	Moderate	Very heavy **X**	Light
Ductus	Thick/sharp	Thin/sharp **X**	Thin/pasty	Thick/pasty
*Tempo	Moderate	Fast **X**	Fairly fast	Slow
Form	Mixed	Oval	Angular **X**	Round
Stability	Moderate **X**	Variable	Regular	Precise
Ltr pattern	Simplified	Elaborated	Copybook **X**	Enlarged
*Height	Moderate	Tall	Small **X**	Moderate
*Width	Moderate	Wide	Narrow **X**	Very wide
*Area Size	1/1/2	2/2/2	3/1/1 **X**	1/2-1-1/2
D/t stem If looped	Short/ narrow	Tall/ narrow	Tall/ **X** wide	Short/ narrow
Total:		1	3	8

_____   _____   _____   _____

*Most important factors for rapid check
Temperament: Phlegmatic/Melancholic

activates their times
my posture will reflect
increased confidence.

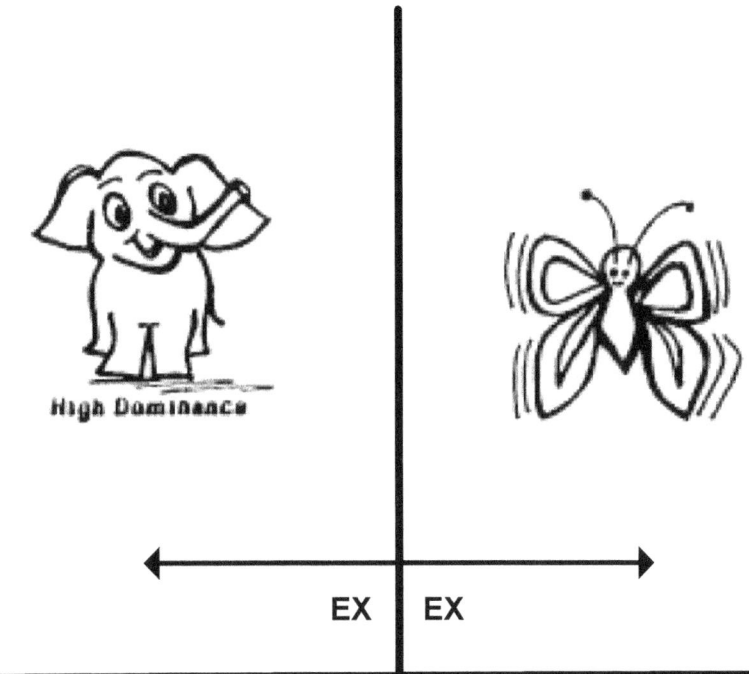

High Dominance

EX | EX

CHOLERIC/SANGUINE (CS)		SANGUINE/CHOLERIC/ (SC)	
second strongest extrovert blend		**second strongest extrovert blend**	
Strengths	**Weaknesses**	**Strengths**	**Weaknesses**
Communicating	Arrogant	Resolute	Angry
Practical	Critical	Outgoing	Talkative
Fearless	Sarcastic	Productive	Obstinate
Energetic	Impatient	Popular	Superficial
Optimistic	Self-sufficient	Independent	Impractical
Sociable	Resentful	Sociable	Opinionated
Empathetic	Hostile	Kindly	Restless
Tolerant	Proud	Spontaneous	Forgetful
Productive	Workaholic	Charismatic	Weak-willed
Highly motivated	Explosive	Happy/fun-loving	Gossipy

CHOLERIC/MELANCHOLIC (CM)

The choleric self-sufficient, unemotional, insensitive attitude is tempered by the melancholic traits of empathy, loyalty and sensitivity

Strengths	Weaknesses
Thorough	Resentful
Optimistic	Sarcastic
Self-sacrificing	Perfectionistic
Leadership	Stubborn
Forceful	Hostile
Successful	Workaholic
Skilled orator	Autocratic
Competitive	Demanding
Industrious	Indolent
Detailed	Prejudiced
Aggressive	Manipulative
Goal-oriented	Impatient
Analytical	Impetuous

EX

IN

MELANCHOLIC/CHOLERIC (MC)

The oversensitive, critical, moody traits of the melancholic are balanced by the enthusiastic optimism of the choleric

Strengths	Weaknesses
Intense	Anxious
Loyal	Irresolute
Gifted	Procrastinating
Self-sacrificing	Suspicious
Zealous	Pessimistic
Soft-hearted	Hostile
Perfectionist	Critical
Capable	Angry/vengeful
Driving	Nitpicking

CHOLERIC/PHLEGMATIC (CP)
(Unexcited, calm extrovert)

The deliberateness and laid-back attitude of the phlegmatic tempers the strong-willed, aggressiveness of the choleric.

Strengths	Weaknesses
Capable	Bullheaded
Deliberate	Sarcastic
Organized	Resentful
Thorough	Inflexible
Unexcited	Unmotivated
Good-humored	Anxious
Calm	Fearful
Efficient	Negative
Subdued	Vengeful
Solitary	Ridiculing

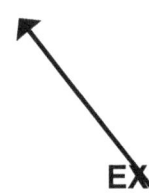

EX

IN

PHLEGMATIC/CHOLERIC (PC)
(Active phlegmatic)

Choleric activity and dynamic strength help to overcome the procrastination, indecision, and phlegmatic lack of motivation.

Strengths	Weaknesses
Practical	Unmotivated
Gentle	Fearful
Quiet	Stubborn
Helpful	Passive
Diplomatic	Self-protective
Thorough	Indecisive
Trustworthy	Withdrawn
Cautious	Lonely
Amiable	Boring
Efficient	Easygoing
Non-threatening	Inflexible

SANGUINE/MELANCHOLIC (SM)
(Most emotional of the temperaments)

The combination of the emotionality of both the sanguine and melancholic creates a soft-hearted, people-oriented person.

Strengths	**Weaknesses**
Empathetic	Irresolute
Cheerful	Worried
Friendly	Critical
Dramatic	Despondent
Perfectionist	Theoretical
Gifted	Negative
Creative	Discouraged
Colorful	Weak-willed
Personable	Egotistical
Enthusiastic	Suspicious

EX

IN

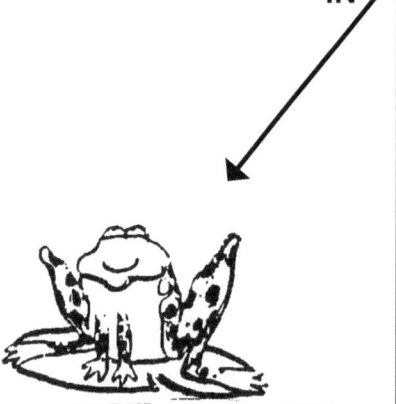

MELANCHOLIC/SANGUINE (MS)
(Most gifted temperament)

The combination of moodiness in both temperaments makes the MS very emotions, like the SM. Their dramatic nature makes them great entertainers and communicators

Strengths	**Weaknesses**
Dramatic	Moody
Detailed	Emotional
Exacting	Uncooperative
Gifted	Self-centered
Soft-hearted	Fearful
Artistic	Idealistic
Well-spoken	Insecure
Self-sacrificing	Self-pitying
Scholastic	Impractical
Musical	Rigid

SANGUINE/PHLEGMATIC (SP)
(Most likable, least extroverted Sanguine)

The qualities of the outgoing sanguine are toned down by the easygoing, faithful phlegmatic.

Strengths	Weaknesses
Good-humored	Mercurial
Enthusiastic	Happy-go-lucky
Gracious	Easygoing
Composed	Unmotivated
Outgoing	Indecisive
Personable	Weak-willed
Diplomatic	Lethargy
Goal-oriented	Procrastinates
Precise	Lethargic

EX

IN

PHLEGMATIC/SANGUINE (PS)
(Non-aggressive, congenial)

This combination melds the good nature of the phlegmatic with the undisciplined phlegmatic temperament–two weaknesses that could lead to inertia.

Strengths	Weaknesses
Outer-directed	Unmotivated
Warm	Undisciplined
Receptive	Indecisive
Peace-loving	Fearful
Practical	Weak-willed
Loyal	Selfish
Humorous	Non-aggressive
Dependable	Non-energetic
Diplomatic	Timid
Calm	Self-defeating

MELANCHOLIC/PHLEGMATIC (MP)
(Double Introvert)

The gloomy, brooding tendencies of the melancholic are tempered by the quiet apathy of the phlegmatic.

Strengths	Weaknesses
Cheerful	Fearful
Good-natured	Anxious
Gifted	Hostile
Analytical	Vengeful
Organized	Overextended
Efficient	Discouraged
Amiable	Workaholic
Quiet	Impractical
Self-sacrificing	Critical
Conscientious	Suspicious

PHLEGMATIC/MELANCHOLIC (PM)
(Quiet, reclusive double introvert)

The gentle, unobtrusive phlegmatic is happy in a life of uninvolvement and peaceful quiet. Non-involvement characterizes this type.

Strengths	Weaknesses
Detailed	Inertia
Organized	Negativism
Quiet	Fear
Neat	Indecision
Diplomatic	Selfish
Steady	Unmotivated
Efficient	Undisciplined
Humorous	Uninvolved
Peace-loving	Unsociable
Composed	Passive

IN   IN

TEMPERAMENT WORKSHEET

FACTOR	Choleric Elephant	Sanguine Butterfly	Melancholic Frog	Phlegmatic Turtle
Gestalt	Dynamic Vital	Restless Expansive	Intense Agitated	Relaxed Calm
Slant	BC -E+	BC - DE	CD-E+	FA-BC
*Pressure	Heavy	Moderate	Very heavy	Light
Ductus	Thick/sharp	Thin/sharp	Thin/pasty	Thick/pasty
*Tempo	Moderate	Fast	Fairly fast	Slow
Form	Mixed	Oval	Angular	Round
Stability	Moderate	Variable	Regular	Precise
Ltr pattern	Simplified	Elaborated	Copybook	Enlarged
*Height	Moderate	Tall	Small	Moderate
*Width	Moderate	Wide	Narrow	Very wide
*Area Size	1/1/2	2/2/2	3/1/1	1/2-1-1/2
D/t stem If looped	Short/ narrow	Tall/ narrow	Tall/ wide	Short/ narrow
Total:	_____	_____	_____	_____

*Most important factors for rapid check
Temperament: Choleric/Melancholic

BIBLIOGRAPHY

Amend, K. & Ruiz, M. Handwriting Analysis. The Complete Basic Book. Newcastle Publishing Co., Inc., North Hollywood, CA 1980.

Bernard, Marie. The Art of Graphology. The Whitston Publishing Company Troy, New York, 1985.

Bruce, Ruth R. Handwriting Analysis· An Introduction. A textbook to advance consistency in handwriting analysis. Blue Clover Publishing, Greeley, CO, i984.

Canoles, June, SND. Find It More Ways, Motivations, Insyte. San Iose, CA i984.

Casewit, Curtis W. Graphology Handbook, Para Research, Ioe., Rockport, Mass., i980.

de Sainte Colombe, Paul. Grapho-Therapeutics. Pen and Pencil Therapy, Grapho-Therapeutics, Hollywood, CA, i980.

Greene, Iames & Lewis, David. The Hidden Language of Your Handwriting. Pan Books, Ltd., London, England, i980.

Handwriting Consultants. Vocational Evaluation Course, Handwriting Consultants, San Diego, CA,

Hartford, Huntington. You Are What You Write. Collier Books, MacMillan, New York, N.Y., i979.

Hearns, Rudolph S. Handwriting, An Analysis Through Its Symbolism, Vantage Press, Inc., New York, N.Y., i979.

Hock, Rev. Conrad. The Four Temperaments, Bruce Publishing Co., Milwaukee,1934.

Kendall, Steve. Interpreting Your Behavioral Style. (Manuscript), Pinole, CA, i985.

King, Leslie W. & Petersen, Christina. Getting Control of Your Life. Handwriting Consultants International, North Salt Lake, Utah, i979.

LaHaye, Tim. Your Temperament: Discover Its Potential. Tyndale House Publishers, Inc., Wheaton, IL, i984.

Matousek, Rose. ABC'S of Handwriting Analysis. Hinsdale, IL., i985 McDermid, Barbara Heinz. Rhythmic Balance Analysis of Handwriting.

Heinz-Grapho, Mountain View, CA, i985.

Mendel, Alfred 0. Personality in Handwriting, Stephen Daye Press, New York, N.Y., i982.

Mills, Coeta. The Professional's Profiling Workbook. C.M. Profiles, Dallas, Tx., 1983.

Roman, Klara G. Handwriting. A Key to Personality. Pantheon Books, New York, N.Y., 1952.

Teillard, Ania. The Soul and Handwriting. A Treatise on Graphology Based on Analytical Psychology. Trans. from the French by Edward B. O'Neill.

Werling, Rev. Norman.   Graphoanalysis. Supplementary Class Notes for the Introductory Course in Graphoanalysis. Compiled by Rev. Norman Werling, Englewood, New Iersey.

Notes from Seminars Presented in Northern California.

Temperament. The Key to Personality as Revealed in Handwriting. GraphoDynamics, Paramus, NI.

Walter Hegar's Basic Stroke Gestalt for Handwriting Analysis. Translated and adapted by Norman Werling, GraphoDynamics, Paramus, NI.

Wheelwright, M.D., Ioseph. Psychological Types, (Manuscript) C.G. Iung Institute of San Francisco Publication, 1973.

Write Choice Ink books

Advanced Studies in Handwriting Psychology, Collected Works of:

Sr. June Canoles
Jeanette Farmer
Terry Henley
Renate Griffiths
Sheila Lowe
Shirl Solomon
Roger Rubin

Non-fiction books by Sheila Lowe

Reading Between the Lines: Decoding Handwriting

Advanced Studies in Handwriting Psychology

Personality & Anxiety Disorders

Succeeding in the Business of Handwriting Analysis

Improve Your Life with Graphotherapy

Handwriting of the Famous & Infamous

The Complete Idiot's Guide to Handwriting Analysis

Sheila Lowe's Handwriting Analyzer software

MEMOIR

Growing From the Ashes

FICTION WORKS BY SHEILA LOWE

CLAUDIA ROSE NOVELS

Poison Pen

Written In Blood

Dead Write

Last Writes

Inkslingers Ball

Outside The Lines

Written Off

Dead Letters

Maximum Pressure

BEYOND THE VEIL NOVELS

What She Saw

Proof Of Life

The Last Door

www.ingramcontent.com/pod-product-compliance
Lightning Source LLC
Chambersburg PA
CBHW051312120626
46547CB00015B/2197